TRANSITION TO ADULTHOOD
Work, Community, and Educational Success

L. Lynn Stansberry Brusnahan
Robert A. Stodden
Stanley H. Zucker
Editors

© 2018 Council for Exceptional Children Division on Autism and Developmental Disabilities

All rights reserved. No part of this publication may be reproduced, stored in a retrieval system, or transmitted, in any form or by any means, electronic, mechanical, photocopying, recording, or otherwise, without prior written permission of the copyright owner.

Council for Exceptional Children
2900 Crystal Drive, Suite 100
Arlington, VA 22202
www.cec.sped.org

Library of Congress Cataloging-in-Publication data

Stansberry Brusnahan, L. Lynn
Transition to Adulthood: Work, Community, and Educational Success
Ed. by L. Lynn Stansberry Brusnahan, Robert A. Stodden, and Stanley H. Zucker.
p. cm.
Includes biographical references.

ISBN 978-0-86586-535-8 (soft cover edition)
ISBN 978-0-86586-536-5 (eBook edition)
CEC Product No. P6296 (soft cover edition)
CEC Product No. P6297 (eBook edition)

Cover design by Tom Karabatakis, Tompromo Marketing

Layout by Tom Karabatakis, Tompromo Marketing

Printed in the United States of America by Sheridan Books, Inc.

First edition

10 9 8 7 6 5 4 3 2 1

Contents

Editors and Contributors v

Introduction 1

Chapter 1
A Framework for Supporting Transition-Age Students 3
Robert A. Stodden, Leslie K. O. Okoji, and Sean Nagamatsu

Chapter 2
Transition Assessment 19
Joshua M. Pulos and James E. Martin

Chapter 3
Transition-Focused Program Plans 35
Kathryn M. Burke, Karrie A. Shogren, and Michael L. Wehmeyer

Chapter 4
Person-Centered Planning, Summary of Performance, and Guardianship 49
L. Lynn Stansberry Brusnahan, Shannon L. Sparks, Debra L. Cote, and Terri Vandercook

Chapter 5
Preparing Students for Inclusive Postschool Settings 67
Leslie K.O. Okoji, Sean Nagamatsu, Robert A. Stodden, and Eric Folk

Chapter 6
Preparing Students for Employment 79
Kathryn K. Yamamoto, Nancy Farnon-Molfenter, and Evan Nakatsuka

Chapter 7
Preparing Students for Postsecondary Education 99
L. Lynn Stansberry Brusnahan, Marc Ellison, and Dedra Hafner

Chapter 8
Community Participation and Supports 125
Emily C. Bouck and Erik W. Carter

Index 145

About the Council for Exceptional Children

The Council for Exceptional Children (CEC) is a professional association of educators dedicated to advancing the success of children with exceptionalities. CEC accomplishes its mission through advocacy, standards, and professional development. CEC represents all disciplines in the field, including teachers, early interventionists, administrators, researchers, and higher education faculty who are preparing the next generation of special educators.

Advocacy

CEC works to ensure that the needs of special educators and early interventionists, and the children and youth they serve, are heard and heeded by policy makers, and engages an active grassroots advocacy network to advance CEC's critical policy messages.

Professional Standards

CEC advances standards that provide benchmarks for developing or revising policy and procedures for program accreditation, entry-level licensure, professional practice, and continuing professional growth.

Professional Resources

CEC supports the vision of well-prepared special educators teaching all children and youth. CEC works to enhance the knowledge, skills, diversity and cultural competency of the profession by providing the resources its members need, including:

- An annual Convention & Expo that is the premier gathering of special and gifted educators and early interventionists in the world.
- *Exceptional Children,* the premier research journal in the field of special education.
- *TEACHING Exceptional Children,* a leading trade publication that translates research into effective classroom practice.

Units and Special Interest Divisions

CEC members network, learn, and share within state and provincial units in the United States and Canada. CEC's 18 special interest divisions focus on the most critical issues in special education: developmental disabilities and autism; behavioral disorders; administration; diagnostic services; communicative disabilities and deafness; cultural and linguistic diversity; early childhood; learning disabilities; physical, health and multiple disabilities; research; global issues; visual and performing arts; career development and transition; visual impairments; gifted education; teacher education; and technology.

Council for Exceptional Children
2900 Crystal Drive, Suite 100
Arlington, VA 22202
888-232-7733
www.cec.sped.org

Editors and Contributors

Editors

L. Lynn Stansberry Brusnahan, Ph.D., is a professor in and chair of the Department of Special Education in the School of Education at the University of St. Thomas in Minnesota, and the parent of a young adult with autism spectrum disorder. Dr. Brusnahan has served on the board of directors of the Autism Society of America and the Council for Exceptional Children's (CEC) Division on Autism and Developmental Disabilities (DADD), and is the co-author of *Do-Watch-Listen-Say: Social and Communication Skills for Autism Spectrum Disorder*. In 2012, she was Autism Society Professional of the Year. Her research focuses on autism spectrum disorder, postsecondary transition, and teacher preparation.

Robert A. Stodden, Ph.D., is Professor Emeritus and Principal Investigator with the Postsecondary Supports Project at the University of Hawai'i at Mānoa. He has more than 35 years of experience working with large-scale evaluation and research projects, as the founding Director of the Center on Disability Studies. Dr. Stodden has served as Chairperson of the Department of Special Education at the University of Hawai'i at Mānoa and Coordinator of Special Needs Graduate Programs at Boston College, and as a principal investigator for more than 100 funded research and training projects. During the 1997 reauthorization of the Individuals With Disabilities Education Act, Dr. Stodden served as a Kennedy Senior Policy Fellow with the U.S. Senate's Disability Policy Subcommittee, drafting and negotiating much of the legislation's transition language. His research focuses on assessing the value of secondary school programs related to in-school and postschool outcomes.

Stanley H. Zucker, Ph.D., is Professor of Special Education in the Division of Educational Leadership and Innovation at Arizona State University. He is the editor of the DADD's research journal, *Education and Training in Autism and Developmental Disabilities*, and of the *DADD Online Journal*. His research focuses on quantitative methods; single subject design; postsecondary transition; foundations, values, and issues in education; social behavior management; assessment and academic achievement of students in English as a Second Language and bilingual programs; and programming for incarcerated youth.

Contributors

Emily C. Bouck, Ph.D., is a professor of special education in the Department of Counseling, Educational Psychology, and Special Education in the College of Education at Michigan State University. Her research focuses on life skills and mathematics curricula for students with disabilities, with a particular focus on students with mild intellectual disability.

Kathryn M. Burke, M.Ed., is a doctoral student in the Department of Special Education at the University of Kansas and Project ACCESS Fellow at the Beach Center on Disability and the Kansas University Center on Developmental Disabilities. Her research focus is self-determination across the lifespan.

Erik W. Carter, Ph.D., is Cornelius Vanderbilt Professor of Special Education in the Department of Special Education at Peabody College, Vanderbilt University, Tennessee. His research focuses on effective strategies for supporting inclusion in school, work, congregational, and community settings for children and adults with intellectual and developmental disabilities.

Debra L. Cote, Ph.D., is an associate professor in the Department of Special Education at California State University, Fullerton (CSUF). She is the associate director of the CSUF Center for Autism, Education Core. Her research focuses on positive behavior support; evidence-based practices for students with autism spectrum disorder; co-teaching and clinical practice; transition, employment, and postschool outcomes; and cultural and linguistic diversity.

Marc Ellison, Ed.D., is a licensed professional counselor and Executive Director of the West Virginia Autism Training Center (WVATC), Marshall University. The WVATC operates the College Program for Students with Autism Spectrum Disorder at Marshall and Concord universities. These on-campus programs support students as they earn a college degree, live, and participate in a campus community, and transition to the workforce. His research focuses on assessing the readiness of institutions of higher education to instruct and support students with autism spectrum disorder.

Nancy Farnon-Molfenter, Ph.D., is Transition Improvement Specialist and Grant Director on the Wisconsin Department of Public Instruction Special Education team. She has worked in the field of special education and disability services for over 25 years as a special educator, and transition coordinator, administrator, and as a grant project consultant for Let's Get to Work and Employment First statewide projects. Her research focuses on transition, employment, and inclusive education that contributes to positive outcomes for all.

Editors and Contributors

Eric Folk, M.Ed., is Principal Investigator of the Postsecondary Supports Projects and the Comprehensive Service Center for People who are Deaf, Hard of Hearing, or Deaf-Blind based at the Center on Disability Studies, University of Hawai'i at Mānoa. His research focuses on self-determination, inclusive postsecondary education, and support provision for people who are deaf or hard of hearing.

Dedra Hafner, Ed.D., is the founder and director of the Cutting Edge Program and an assistant professor at Edgewood College, Wisconsin. Since 2007, Cutting Edge has supported and provided students with disabilities the opportunity to attend college. In 2013, she received the Inclusive Education Award from TASH. Her research focuses on inclusion in postsecondary education and identifying and addressing barriers to inclusion of individuals with significant disabilities in college.

James E. Martin, Ph.D., is Emeritus Zarrow Family Professor and retired Director of the University of Oklahoma's Zarrow Center for Learning Enrichment. He and colleagues developed the Transition Assessment and Goal Generator, and the Transition Assessment and Goal Generator-Alternate for use with students with significant cognitive disabilities. Dr. Martin's past works include the ChoiceMaker Self-Determination Assessment and Lesson packages and the *Self-Directed Supported Employment Handbook*, along with dozens of articles and book chapters. His research focuses on the transition of youth with disabilities from high school to postsecondary education through the application of self-determination assessment and instructional practices.

Sean Nagamatsu, M.Ed, M.L.I.Sc., is an instructional and student support staff member with the Postsecondary Support Project and the Center on Disability Studies at the University of Hawai'i at Mānoa. He taught English at Wai'anae High School and worked with students at Kapi'olani, Honolulu, and Leeward Community Colleges, as part of the Postsecondary Support Project.

Evan Nakatsuka, M.Ed., is the project coordinator for the Postsecondary Support Project contract with the Hawai'i Division of Vocational Rehabilitation and is a faculty team leader for the Hawai'i Postsecondary Support Project. He has been working in the field of vocational rehabilitation and disability services for 8 years, and has worked as a job developer, program manager, and administrator for a local community rehabilitation provider.

Leslie K. O. Okoji, Ph.D., is an assistant specialist at the Center on Disability Studies at the University of Hawai'i at Mānoa. She has over 20 years of experience working in the field of education, primarily as a school counselor in public secondary schools. Dr. Okoji currently serves as an evaluator on the HI-AWARE and No Wrong Door projects at the Center on Disability Studies.

Joshua M. Pulos is a Sooner Scholar, pursuing his doctorate in special education with an emphasis in applied behavior analysis and secondary transition education at the University of Oklahoma's Zarrow Center for Learning Enrichment. In October 2015, the Council for Exceptional Children's Division on Career Development and Transition awarded Mr. Pulos the Andrew Halpern Early Career Practitioner Award. His research interests include behavior–analytic interventions to promote positive postsecondary outcomes of students with disabilities, intellectual and developmental disabilities, self-determination, sexuality and disability, and transition assessment.

Karrie A. Shogren, Ph.D., is Professor and Director of the Kansas University Center on Developmental Disabilities. Her research focuses on self-determination and systems of supports for adolescents and adults with disabilities.

Shannon L. Sparks, Ph.D., is an assistant professor in the Department of Special Education, Rehabilitation and Counseling at California State University, San Bernardino. Her research interests include teaching choice-making to students with mild and moderate disabilities, postsecondary education and gender outcomes, evidence-based practices for students with autism spectrum disorder, and guardianship.

Terri Vandercook, Ph.D., is Assistant Director of the National Technical Assistance Center on Inclusive Practices and Policies for Students With Significant Cognitive Disabilities. She previously was an associate professor and chair of the Department of Special Education at the University of St. Thomas in Minnesota and coordinator for the program in Developmental Disabilities. Her interests include inclusive schooling, collaborative teaming, instruction of students with significant cognitive disabilities, and teacher training.

Michael L. Wehmeyer, Ph.D., is Ross and Marianna Beach Distinguished Professor in Special Education, Chair of the Department of Special Education, and Director and Senior Scientist of the Beach Center on Disability, all at the University of Kansas. His research interests include self-determination, applications of positive psychology to disability, and transition to adulthood for youth with intellectual and developmental disabilities.

Kathryn K. Yamamoto, Ph.D., is an associate professor and director of the University of Hawai'i at Mānoa's Rehabilitation Counselor Education Program. Dr. Yamamoto has worked in the field of vocational rehabilitation and disability services for over 30 years. Her research interests are grounded in her employment history, which reveals a passion for working with persons with disabilities and includes serving as a vocational rehabilitation counselor, transition specialist, and project director for the Transition Program for Students With Intellectual Disabilities in Hawai'i.

Introduction

The Prism series, developed by the Council for Exceptional Children's Division on Autism and Developmental Disabilities, is a collection of volumes that highlight evidence-based research-to-practice teaching strategies and interventions geared toward supporting students with autism spectrum disorder (ASD) and other developmental disabilities (DD). The volumes in the Prism collection address interventions in the classroom, home, and community and focus on how to help students build needed skills.

Prism Volume 11 focuses on the transition from being a student in high school to an adult functioning in society. The eight chapters in this volume, written by 20 authors, highlight preparation for and transition from the secondary environment to postsecondary education, employment, and community involvement. The target population highlighted in this volume is individuals with developmental disabilities, including those with ASD and intellectual disability (ID). The target audience for this volume include special education teachers, general education teachers, secondary school professionals, transition personnel, Department of Education personnel, vocational rehabilitation counselors, and individuals with disabilities along with their families. The authors discuss a range of approaches and models currently being used, and the current status on postschool life for young people with developmental disabilities.

Chapter 1 ("A Framework for Supporting Transition-Age Students") provides readers with a background on the topic of transition as it relates to youth with DD, including those with ASD and ID. The authors present data and information in support of the transition initiative, illustrating its value to young persons in the target population and the educators and others who play supporting roles in this process. This chapter highlights the history of advocacy and legislative efforts that drove the creation of the transition planning and preparation requirements in the Individuals With Disabilities Education Act, within the historical context of this initiative.

Chapter 2 ("Transition Assessment") provides a historical lens to better understand students with disabilities and the grassroots philosophical undertaking prompting the transition movement. The authors offer guidance on principles that inform the transition assessment process for youth with DD and an overview of some of the most commonly used assessment approaches and tools.

Chapter 3 ("Transition-Focused Program Plans") illustrates how transition plans can be used to support youth with DD as they move from school to the adult world. The authors take a closer look at transition planning and introduce evidence-based strategies that enhance the planning process.

Chapter 4 ("Person-Centered Planning, Summary of Performance, and Guardianship") highlights the essential elements of person-centered planning, summary of performance, and guardianship practices. The authors provide information to assist readers in playing a key role in these processes and enhance the successful transition from high school to adult functioning for individuals with DD.

Chapter 5 ("Preparing Students for Inclusive Postschool Settings") focuses on the importance and significance of inclusive settings in and beyond high schools for youth with DD. The authors present a best-practice framework to support transition to inclusive postschool options, and suggest strategies that lead to inclusive skill development and successful transition to postschool settings.

Chapter 6 ("Preparing Students for Employment") describes the central collaborators who provide employment services and should be involved in the planning and service provision process. The authors provide an overview of evidence-based strategies and best practices that promote and support competitive integrated employment outcomes for students with DD.

Chapter 7 ("Preparing Students for Postsecondary Education") describes some of the benefits of participation in continuing education for individuals with disabilities and a variety of higher education options. The authors discuss some of the barriers to success and highlight effective practices to prepare students with disabilities for higher education.

Chapter 8 ("Community Participation and Supports") focuses on the topic of community-based instruction and the real-life skills that youth with DD need to master in order to live as independently as possible and function successfully in an inclusive society. The authors discuss community-based instruction as a format to bridge community participation with instructional preparation and have individuals learn skills in natural settings.

CHAPTER 1
A Framework for Supporting Transition-Age Students
Robert A. Stodden, Leslie K. O. Okoji, and Sean Nagamatsu

Objectives:
- Introduce the topic of transition.
- Provide background and rationale concerning transition.
- Present key terms and legislation supporting transition initiatives.

Chapter 1 provides an overview of the topic of postsecondary transition as it relates to youth with developmental disabilities, including those with autism spectrum disorder and intellectual disability, and the role of educators and others in this process. This chapter provides historical background and information regarding the transition initiative, illustrating its value to individuals with disabilities, and the history of advocacy and legislative efforts leading to the transition planning and preparation requirements of the Individuals With Disabilities Education Act (IDEA, 2006).

Key Terminology	
Autism spectrum disorder	A developmental disability significantly affecting verbal and nonverbal communication and social interaction, generally evident before age 3, that adversely affects a child's educational performance. Other characteristics often associated with ASD are engagement in repetitive activities and stereotyped movements, resistance to environmental change or change in daily routines, and unusual responses to sensory experiences. (See 34 CFR § 300.8[c][1].)

Key Terminology (cont'd)	
Developmental disability	A severe, chronic disability attributed to a mental or physical impairment that is manifested during childhood or youth and which is likely to continue indefinitely. A developmental disability results in substantial functional limitations in a major life activity (i.e., self-care, receptive and expressive living, economic self-sufficiency) and requires individualized support services. (See 42 U.S.C. § 12102[1].)
Individualized education program	A plan that guides the education of a student with a disability who has been found eligible for special education services. In addition to regulatory language and protections of student rights, the IEP must include: • appropriate measurable postsecondary goals based upon age-appropriate transition assessments related to training, education, employment and, where appropriate, independent living skills; and • transition services needed in order to reach those goals. (See 34 CFR 300.320[b][c].) The student must be invited to attend the IEP team meeting if the team is planning on discussing or establishing postsecondary goals and identifying needed transition services. (See 34 CFR § 300.321[b].)
Intellectual disability	Significantly below average general intellectual functioning, existing concurrently with deficits in adaptive behavior and manifested during the developmental period, that adversely affects a child's educational performance. (See 34 CFR § 300.8[c][6].)

Key Terminology (cont'd)	
Transition services	A coordinated set of activities for a student with a disability that: • is designed to be within a results-oriented process, that is focused on improving the academic and functional achievement of the child with a disability to facilitate the child's movement from school to post-school activities, including postsecondary education, vocational education, integrated employment (including supported employment); continuing and adult education, adult services, independent living, or community participation; • is based on the individual child's needs, taking into account the child's strengths, preferences, and interests; and includes (i) instruction; (ii) related services; (iii) community experiences; (iv) the development of employment and other post-school adult living objective; and (v) if appropriate, acquisition of daily living skills and functional vocational evaluation. (See 34 CFR § 300.43[a])

Transition—including the transition from secondary school to adulthood—is a sequence of events and life changes (endings and beginnings) that all youth undertake. All young people require various levels of support when transitioning to adult roles in postsecondary education, independent community living, and valued employment. Youth with disabilities often require additional supports and services with preparation for, linkage to, and assistance being received and accepted within these various adult roles.

In the early 1980s, Madeline Will, then Assistant Secretary of the Office of Special Education and Rehabilitative Services (OSERS), sought to frame a model of providing support to youth with significant disabilities who were preparing to transition from secondary school to roles in adult employment (Will, 1984; see Figure 1.1). This framework recognizes that each person has diverse support needs as they prepare for and make transitions. The model clusters these needs into three different levels of service delivery: (a) no services are needed at this time; (b) time-limited services are required, some more important than others; and (c) ongoing or continuous provision of services is required. This model focused solely

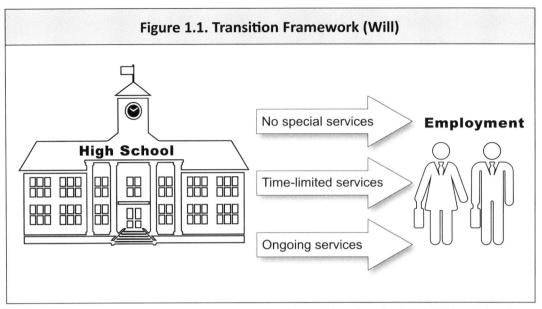

Figure 1.1. Transition Framework (Will)

Note. Reprinted and adapted from "OSERS Programming for the Transition of Youth With Disabilities: Bridges From School to Work," by M. Will, 1983, p. 7. Copyright 1983 by Office of Special Education and Rehabilitative Services.

upon employment as an outcome, leading to concern that other outcomes such as independent community living and recreation or leisure roles needed also to be considered in planning for the transition from high school to adulthood.

As the transition initiative took hold in high schools across the nation during the mid- to late 1980s, there was increased interest in further defining and specifying how transition activities should be carried out with students with disabilities. Andrew Halpern (1985) voiced a need for thinking broadly about the transition process. He built upon Will's framework by recognizing that community adjustment was a critical filter that each person with a disability had to pass through successfully on their way to participation in adult roles such as employment (see Figure 1.2). Halpern recognized that focusing only on employment was too narrow of an approach when developing a transition plan or when carrying out transition activities.

The development of various transition support frameworks and models was followed throughout the 1980s and early 1990s with federally funded projects focused on demonstrating transition supports for young persons with all types of disabilities. The outcomes of these projects, as well as an Office of Special Education Programs (OSEP) report focused on the devastating postschool outcomes experienced by youth with disabilities leaving secondary school, led to the first steps to include legislative language which directly spoke to the transition needs of youth with disabilities. Historically, groundbreaking policy or legislative language regarding this transition included changes or additions to (a) Public Law

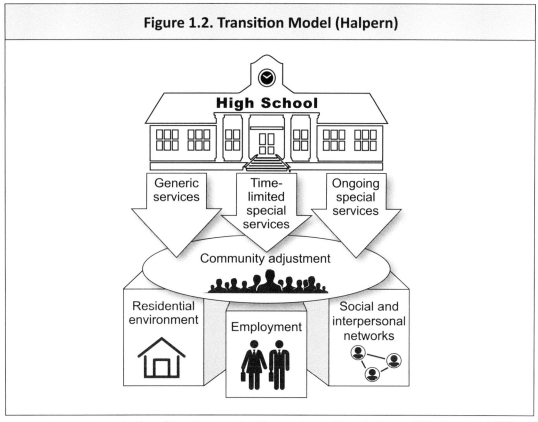

Note. Reprinted and adapted from "Transition: A Look at the Foundations," by A. S. Halpern, 1985, *Exceptional Children, 51*, p. 480. Copyright 1985 by the Council for Exceptional Children.

94-142 (reauthorized as IDEA), which focuses on quality preparation in secondary school and transition linkage to postsecondary education and employment; (b) the Americans With Disabilities Act of 1990 (reauthorized as the ADA Amendments Act of 2008), which focuses on providing reasonable accommodations and ensuring equal access to learning and work environments; and (c) Section 504 of the Rehabilitation Act of 1973, which provides financial assistance and training support leading to quality employment and independent community living.

Most important as a legal mandate is IDEA. Specifically, the IDEA amendments of 1997 and its reauthorization in 2004 legislated obligations regarding the provision of transition services on the part of state and local education agencies. These requirements were put into place to ensure students with all disabilities greater access to the core general education curriculum and state and local accountability assessment systems. IDEA amendments also expanded previous transition requirements by requiring that an individualized education program (IEP) include, at age 14 or earlier, a statement of transition service needs focused on the student's course of study (e.g., participation in Advanced Placement courses or vocational education programs). The IEP was also to include, beginning at age 16 or younger, identification of key players to provide needed transition services and interagency responsibilities or any necessary linkages. These legislative requirements were made on the assumption that challenging all students academically would result in more responsive teaching and learning, as well as improved academic and transition outcomes (see Table 1.1).

Legislative changes in this area have often been led by the persistence and commitment of family members and self-advocates with disabilities. As advocacy provided the pressure and context for legislative changes, it also triggered a rethinking of who persons with disabilities were and how they should be addressed and supported. This paradigm shift in how persons with disabilities were viewed, labeled, and supported initially evolved out of the deinstitutionalization movement of the 1960s and 1970s, where services were often decided upon and provided within the context of the medical model. With the intense and combative work of self-advocates and family members, movement toward use of "person-first" language, use of less stigmatizing labels (e.g., *person with intellectual disability* rather than *mentally retarded*), and strategies for empowering individuals with disabilities to determine their own futures became an expectation of everyone in the field.

The importance of quality secondary school preparation and early interagency transition services for youth with disabilities has been emphasized in the literature for several decades (Folk, Yamamoto, & Stodden, 2012; Johnson, Sharpe, & Stodden, 2000; Johnson & Thurlow, 2003; Policy Information Clearinghouse, 1997; Stodden & Dowrick, 2000a, 2000b; Stodden & Mrazek, 2010), and is directly linked to improved life opportunities for such youth. Further, preparation for transition to postsecondary and other continuing education opportunities has been hailed as a critical step towards the advancement of positive life outcomes for students with developmental disabilities, autism spectrum disorder, and intellectual disability (Stodden, Abhari, & Kong, 2015). Postsecondary education is an age-appropriate experience for youth with disabilities that is linked directly to increased earnings over a lifetime (Carnevale, Rose, & Cheah, 2011), better employment outcomes in general (Getzel, 2014), and higher quality independent community living (Kleinert, Jones, Sheppard-Jones, Harp, & Harrison, 2012; Schley et al., 2011). Without postsecondary education, employment options for people with disabilities are very limited, with few being competitively paid and many more placed in sheltered settings earning less than the minimum wage (Grigal & Hart, 2013).

Recent federal initiatives and the development of inclusive curricula in secondary schools have increased opportunities for more students to participate in programs in postsecondary schools (Papay & Bambara, 2011). Improved support for secondary educators, comprehensive transition planning, and critical interagency partnerships between secondary schools, employers, parents, students, and postsecondary institutions have helped to ignite new research and

Table 1.1. Key Legislation Pertaining to Transition and Employment

Legislation	Description
Individuals With Disabilities Education Act (IDEA)	IDEA is the primary federal legislation shaping transition services provided by schools to students with disabilities (Etscheidt, 2006; Prince, Katsiyannis, & Farmer, 2013). With each reauthorization of this law came more salient requirements for incorporating transition planning and supports intended to facilitate competitive integrated employment (Prince et al., 2013).
	The State Performance Plan Part B Indicator 13 (34 CFR §300.602) dictates the development of a transition plan, including measurable postschool goals, for each student with an IEP no later than age 16; a number of states have elected to require that transition planning begin by age 14. Goals must be based on the results of age-appropriate transition assessment as well as the student's preferences, interests, needs, and strengths.
	Local education agencies, or school districts, may offer transition services beyond 12th grade when deemed appropriate and necessary by the IEP team.
Americans With Disabilities Act (ADA)	ADA prohibits discrimination and ensures equal opportunity for persons with disabilities in employment, state and local government services, public accommodations, commercial facilities, and transportation.
	ADA (later, the ADA Amendments Act of 2008) prohibits employment discrimination based on disability, instead dictating consideration of the ability of the person to complete job duties. ADA also requires employers to provide reasonable accommodations on the job, which might include but is not limited to adding physical accessibility, restructuring job duties, modifying work schedule, adapting training and work materials, and allowing the use of equipment or assistive technology.

Note. IEP = individualized education program.

model demonstration programs (Folk et al., 2012; Stodden & Dowrick, 2000a; Test et al., 2009). One example of this movement was the creation of model demonstration programs funded through the Department of Education's Office of Postsecondary Education for 5-year periods in 2010 and 2015. The Transition and Postsecondary Education Program for Students With Intellectual Disabilities awarded grants to 27 postsecondary institutions to create or enhance inclusive opportunities for students with developmental and intellectual disabilities in 2010, with another 25 grants awarded in 2015 to expand or develop programs (see National Coordinating Center, 2017, for a visual of current programs).

These projects, as well as other transition demonstration efforts over the years, have informed the development of new frameworks, evidence-based strategies, and best practices which support students with disabilities as they progress toward their transition to postsecondary education and into valued adult roles in the community. Applying what has been learned over the past decade, researchers, program developers, practitioners, and self-advocates have banded together to develop a more comprehensive model transition framework which meets the needs of all persons with disabilities to successfully make the school-to-adult transition. This framework consists of an authentic, inclusive support structure based upon an individualized plan that includes the necessary supports for access and participation in inclusive academic, social, and independent community living, and includes career and vocational activities as students move forward toward valued adult roles. The framework (see Figure 1.3) includes activities which reflect evidence-based strategies known to support the successful transition of youth with significant needs. (This framework also serves as a blueprint for the structure of this PRISM volume, with chapters organized and developed in a manner reflecting these components and strategies.)

Effective Transition Practices

Effective transition practices are grounded within empirical evidence that indicates that (a) serving transition-age students with disabilities in inclusive settings with their same-age peers is the best approach (Uditsky & Hughson, 2012), (b) enhancing a student's self-determination skills leads to improved transition outcomes (Test et al., 2009), and (c) providing opportunities to acquire skills within natural settings contributes to the emergence of self-determined behaviors (Simmons-Reed, Cullen, Day, Izzo, & Colebaugh, 2013). As students transition from secondary school to adulthood, it is important to expand awareness, exploration, and skill development through person-centered planning. Utilizing a person-centered focus for students and families can help them to fully engage and explore postschool options. As illustrated in Figure 1.3, the path to success in transition includes academic, social, and employment preparation: transition planning and preparation, transition experience, and participation in adult roles.

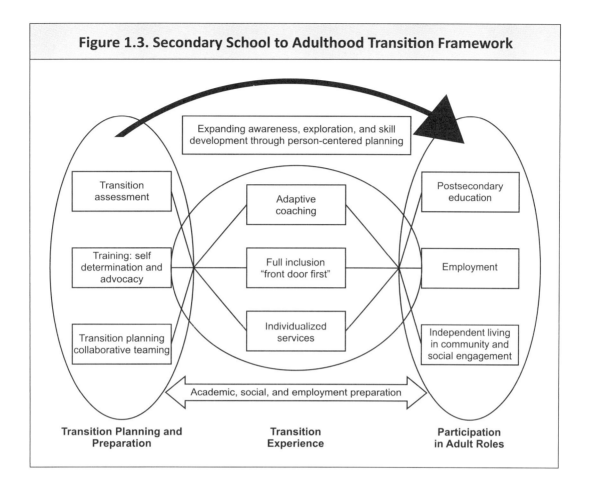

Figure 1.3. Secondary School to Adulthood Transition Framework

Transition Planning and Preparation

Transition planning and preparation should start early in secondary school and include (a) transition assessment; (b) training, including self-determination and advocacy skills; and (c) collaborative teaming. Awareness, exploration, and skill development during transition planning and preparation includes activities such as utilizing person-centered planning (see Chapter 4); reviewing the various expectations regarding the transition; analyzing the costs and benefits of preparation activities; completing application processes; attending information and orientation meetings; and participating in academic, social, independent community living, and vocational activities as they take place in postschool settings.

Transition assessment. An important part of transition planning and preparation includes assessments conducted by secondary schools to determine student preferences, interests, needs, and strengths (see Chapter 2). Based upon these assessments as well as the student's self-determined goals, a person-centered inclusive support plan is developed describing the supports needed. Transition plans (see Chapter 3) can include typical or natural supports, services, accommodations, disability-related supports, and individualized services. Transition assessments can contribute to a comprehensive summary of performance for use in postsecondary environments (see Chapter 4).

Training. Transition planning and preparation includes teaching students the skills they need to meet their transition goals. All students need to build self-determination and self-advocacy skills; training on these skills should be a key focus of comprehensive transition preparation. *Self-determination* is a student engaging in setting and attaining goals, and using skills such as decision making, problem solving, and self-regulation (Shogren, 2013; see Chapter 3). *Self-advocacy* is a student engaging in activity to influence decisions. Teaching self-determination and self-advocacy helps students learn to speak up for themselves. Self-advocates know their rights and responsibilities and make decisions about their own lives. They understand who is there to support them in their journey and reach out to others when they need help.

Collaborative teaming. Comprehensive transition plans are designed through a collaborative teaming approach with key agency involvement (see Chapter 3). Comprehensive transition programming adopts collaborative teaming early in the preparation process to connect students, families, schools, and agencies. Collaborative teaming helps align services and supports to enhance access, participation, and success in inclusive roles to improve education, employment, and independent community living outcomes for students with disabilities.

The Transition Experience

Transition experience is another key component to planning and preparation and includes providing inclusive opportunities, individualized services, and adaptive coaching.

Inclusive opportunities. Applying the "front door first" approach to the transition experience prioritizes student access to inclusive, typical pathways to postschool participation in age-appropriate roles, using natural supports. It assumes the inclusion of resources available to all students before pursuing or providing specialized services. This approach promotes inclusion, authenticity, and self-advocacy in youth with disabilities, and facilitates institutional awareness about the presence and needs of diverse learners on postsecondary campuses, in places of employment, and in local communities (Folk et al., 2012). Chapter 5 focuses on the importance and significance of inclusive opportunities.

Individualized services. For transition experiences to be truly meaningful, the services provided must be based on students' individual needs. One way secondary schools can support students with disabilities throughout the transition process is by assisting them with understanding the differences between postschool settings and high school, and by seeking out the vast array of support systems in postschool settings such as college campuses or places of employment. Helping students identify and learn about various resources and natural supports can positively influence student and family expectations of participating in these settings and can broaden a student's outlook on their future (Folk et al., 2012). Planned activities such as campus and community visits can assist students in familiarizing themselves with navigating the physical layout, as well as learning how to travel independently. Equally important is teaching students appropriate and effective social interaction, communication, and self-advocacy skills to identify and seek out assistance on their own.

Adaptive coaches. Adaptive coaches (see Chapters 5 and 7) are a key component of transition support for students with disabilities. Coaches work with students at an individual or small group level and help students advocate, pursue, and achieve their postschool goals. This includes coaching students in academic and nonacademic social, communication, organization, independence, and self-advocacy skills. At the secondary school level, the specific strategies used by adaptive coaches may be incorporated into the general education classroom setting by teachers, aides, or even trained peers. Specific coaching strategies might include the use of scripts for requesting needed assistance, prompts in the classroom, and preteaching main concepts. Natural supports in the classroom can also provide a wealth of resources to both students with and without disabilities.

Participation in Adult Roles

Participation in adult roles is another key component to the framework and includes postsecondary education, independent community living skills, and integrated employment.

Postsecondary education. Postsecondary education (see Chapter 7) contributes to more positive life outcomes for students with disabilities. Students with disabilities may require assistance in specific academic areas to support their learning in these settings, such as supporting understanding of course content, developing test-taking strategies, learning and memory strategies, and helping students understand the expectations of the course (e.g., reviewing syllabus and materials). Educators need to teach and encourage students to seek additional academic supports through "front door first" options, before seeking disability service options in their campus or community setting.

Independent community living. Students' independent community living skills need to be assessed, in order to identify areas of skill development. Based on these needs, educators should teach students skills and how to utilize them in community setting so they can function as independently as possible. This may involve teaching real-world skills (e.g., community participation, personal health and safety). Specific skills that are critical for students to lead a more independent life include learning to use public transportation or to drive, financial literacy, and housing options. Chapter 4 highlights adult circle of supports, which can be used to support community living. Chapter 8 focuses on strategies to increase the capacity and commitment of communities to meaningfully include individuals with disabilities.

Integrated employment support. It is important to emphasize the connection between school and employment (see Chapter 6) and constantly reinforce skills needed for integrative employment. Assessments and experiences can help students explore employment areas around their own interests and needs and assist them in researching employment outlook, determining skills needed, and calculating expected rate of pay. Youth with disabilities ready for employment should be encouraged to visit school career centers and other employment agencies in their community for additional support.

Summary

The provision of transition services and supports for youth with disabilities has a long history. Advocates, family members, and program developers have worked for many years to build program models, draft legislation, and develop evidence-based strategies which support youth with disabilities to successfully transition from secondary special education environments to valued adult roles in their community. This chapter has provided the reader with an overview and rationale in support of the transition initiative, forming the basis for in-depth discussions in future chapters of evidence-based strategies, approaches, and models which promote a successful and productive transition to postschool life by young persons with disabilities.

References

ADA Amendments Act of 2008, Pub. L. No. 110-325, 122 Stat. 3553, to be codified at 42 U.S.C. § 12101 (2009).

Carnevale, A. P., Rose, S. J., & Cheah, B. (2011). *The college payoff: Education, occupations, lifetime earnings.* Washington, DC: Georgetown University Center on Education and the Workforce. Retrieved from https://www2.ed.gov/policy/highered/reg/hearulemaking/2011/collegepayoff.pdf

Developmental Disabilities Assistance and Bill of Rights Act of 2000, Pub. L. 106-402, 114 Stat. 1677, to be codified at 45 U.S.C. § 15001 *et seq.* (2000)

Etscheidt, S. (2006). Issues in transition planning: Legal decisions. *Career Development for Exceptional Individuals, 29*, 28–47. doi:10.1177/08857288060290010201

Folk, E. R., Yamamoto, K. K., & Stodden, R. A. (2012). Implementing inclusion and collaborative teaming in a model program of postsecondary education for young adults with intellectual disabilities. *Journal of Policy & Practice in Intellectual Disabilities, 9*, 257–269. doi:10.1111/jppi.12007

Getzel, E. E. (2014). United States Congress, Senate Committee on Health, Education, Labor and Pensions: Introductory remarks. *Journal of Vocational Rehabilitation, 40*, 183–184.

Grigal, M., & Hart, D. (2013) Transition and postsecondary education programs for students with intellectual disability: A pathway to employment. *Think College Fast Facts, Issue No. 4.* Boston, MA: University of Massachusetts Boston, Institute for Community Inclusion. Retrieved from https://thinkcollege.net/resource/student-outcomes/transition-and-postsecondary-education-programs-students-intellectual

Halpern, A. S. (1985). Transition: A look at the foundations. *Exceptional Children, 51*, 479–486. doi:10.1177/001440298505100604

IDEA regulations, 34 C.F.R. § 300 (2012).

Individuals With Disabilities Education Act, 20 U.S.C. §§ 1400 *et seq*. (2006 & Supp. V. 2011)

Johnson, D. R., Sharpe, M., & Stodden, R. (2000). The transition to postsecondary education for students with disabilities. *Impact, 13(1), 2–3.* Minneapolis: University of Minnesota, Institute on Community Integration.

Johnson, D. R., & Thurlow, M. L. (2003). *A national study on graduation requirements and diploma options (Technical Report 36).* Minneapolis: University of Minnesota Institute on Community Integration, National Center on Secondary Education and Transition and National Center on Educational Outcomes.

Kleinert, H. L., Jones, M. M., Sheppard-Jones, K., Harp, B., & Harrison, E. M. (2012). Students with intellectual disabilities going to college? Absolutely! *TEACHING Exceptional Children, 44*, 26–35. doi:10.1177/004005991204400503

National Coordinating Center. (2017). *Transition and postsecondary education programs for students with intellectual disabilities.* Retrieved from http://www.thinkcollege.net/about-us/think-college-grant-projects/national-coordinating-center

Papay, C. K., & Bambara, L. M. (2011). Postsecondary education for transition-age students with intellectual and other developmental disabilities: A national survey. *Education and Training in Autism and Developmental Disabilities, 46*, 78–93.

Policy Information Clearinghouse. (1997). Students with disabilities and high school graduation policies. *Policy Update, 5*(6). Alexandria, VA: National Association of State Boards of Education.

Prince, A. M. T., Katsiyannis, A., & Farmer, J. (2013). Postsecondary transition under IDEA 2004: A legal review. *Intervention in School and Clinic, 48*, 286–293. doi:10.1177/1053451212472233

Rehabilitation Act of 1973, as amended by Pub. L. No. 110-325, to be codified at 29 U.S.C. § 701 (2009).

Rosa's Law, Pub. L. 111–256, 124 Stat. 2643, to be codified at 20 U.S.C. §§ 1140 *et seq.* (2010)

Schley, S., Walter, G. G., Weathers, R. R., Hemmeter, J., Hennessey, J. C., & Burkhauser, R. V. (2011). Effect of postsecondary education on the economic status of persons who are deaf or hard of hearing. *Journal of Deaf Studies and Deaf Education, 16*, 524–536. doi:10.1093/deafed/enq060

Shogren, K. A. (2013). *Self-determination and transition planning*. Baltimore, MD: Paul H. Brookes.

Simmons-Reed, E. A., Cullen, J. M., Day, K. J., Izzo, M. V., & Colebaugh, L. B. (2013). Voices of self-determined students with intellectual and developmental disabilities in postsecondary settings. *Research to Practice in Self-Determination Series, 6*, 2–4.

Stodden, R. A., Abhari, K., & Kong, E. (2015). Secondary school preparation and transition of youth with disabilities. In B. G. Cook, M. Tankersley, & T. J. Landrum (Eds.), *Transition of youth and young adults* (pp. 7–30). Bingley, England: Emerald.

Stodden, R. A., & Dowrick, P. W. (2000a). The present and future of postsecondary education for adults with disabilities. *Impact, 13*(1), 4–5.

Stodden, R. A., & Dowrick, P. W. (2000b). Postsecondary education and quality employment for adults with disabilities. *American Rehabilitation, 25*(3), 19–23.

Stodden, R. A., & Mrazek, D. W. (2010). An introduction: Transition to postsecondary education and employment of persons with autism and intellectual disabilities. *Focus on Autism and Other Developmental Disabilities, 25*, 131–133. doi:10.1177/ 1088357610371637

Test, D. W., Fowler, C. H., Richter, S. M., White, J., Mazzotti, V., Walker, A. R., ... Kortering, L. (2009). Evidence-based practices in secondary transition. *Career Development for Exceptional Individuals, 32*, 115–128. 10.1177/0885728809336859

Uditsky, B., & Hughson, E. (2012). Inclusive postsecondary education-an evidence-based moral imperative. *Journal of Policy & Practice in Intellectual Disabilities, 9*, 298–302. doi:10.1111/jppi.12005

Will, M. (1984). *OSERS programming for the transition of youth with disabilities: From school to working life*. Washington, DC: U.S. Department of Education, Office of Special Education and Rehabilitative Services. Retrieved from https://files.eric.ed.gov/fulltext/ED256132.pdf

CHAPTER 2
Transition Assessment
Joshua M. Pulos and James E. Martin

Objectives:
- Define transition assessment and legal requirements.
- Identify resources for transition assessments.
- Define formal and informal transition assessment.
- Present repeated measures situational assessment steps.

"We study the past to understand the present; we understand the present to guide the future" (William Lund, 1886–1971, as quoted by Webster, n.d., p. 2). Chapter 2 provides a historical lens to better understand students with disabilities and the grassroots philosophical undertaking prompting the transition movement. This chapter also reviews guiding principles that inform the transition assessment process for youth with developmental disabilities, including those with autism spectrum disorder and intellectual disability.

Key Terminology	
Formal assessment	A standardized instrument for measuring an array of items that includes descriptions of their norming process, reliability, validity, recommended use, reading level, and direction of administration (see National Technical Assistance Center on Transition, 2016; Neubert & Leconte, 2013).
Informal assessment	A nonstandardized instrument lacking formal norming processes, reliability, and validity information (Neubert & Leconte, 2013).

Key Terminology (cont'd)	
Repeated measures situational assessment	An assessment process where students make choices and repeat the choice making until consistent choices emerge, at which point students are matched to opportunities based on their self-identified preferences (Martin, Woods, Sylvester, & Gardner, 2005).
Transition assessment	An ongoing process of collecting information on students' "preferences, interests, needs, and strengths as they relate to measureable postsecondary goals and the annual goals that will help facilitate attainment of postsecondary goals" (Neubert & Leconte, 2013, pp. 74–75).

For generations, people regarded individuals with disabilities as objects of pity and despair; society deemed them as incompetent to participate or contribute to the community in which they lived (Ward, 1988; Wolfensberger, 1972). Prior to the 20th century, the collective mindset considered these individuals flawed, necessitating segregated institutional services and care to survive (Funk, 1987). Through this perception, state and national policies highlighted the perceived dependence of these individuals and called on welfare and benevolent organizations to take care of the "disabled" (Ward, 1988). Because of these actions, individuals with disabilities were excluded from the workforce as they were viewed as incapable of working. Little thought was given to the idea that these individuals were indeed being discriminated against (Funk, 1987).

Despite grassroots policy efforts in the 1950s and early 1960s to integrate individuals with significant support needs into the community, public attitudes produced an isolating effect (Ward, 1988). However, with even minimal integration into the community, the social status of individuals with disabilities improved. This helped to reduce the marginalization and stigmatization experienced by individuals with disabilities, although it did not end seclusion and segregation. In addition, the tone of the civil rights movement during the late 1960s momentously influenced the disability rights movement. As Funk (1987) affirmed, individuals with disabilities began to receive opportunities to develop autonomy of choice and freedom to belong to and take part in their community.

Grounding Transition Assessment Through Philosophic Orientation

A set of beliefs or philosophic orientation is necessary when providing a framework to successfully support students with disabilities transitioning from high school

Chapter 2

to postsecondary life (Pancsofar & Blackwell, 1986). Thus, this chapter presents the guiding principles that paved the way to more inclusive educational and community settings. These foundational principles include (a) the principle of normalization (Wolfensberger, 1972), (b) the criterion of ultimate functioning (Brown, Nietupski, & Hamre-Nietupski, 1976), and (c) bridges from school to working life (Will, 1983). (See Figure 2.1).

Principle of Normalization

Wolfensberger (1972) defined *normalization* as the "utilization of means which are as culturally normative as possible in order to establish and/or maintain personal behaviors and characteristics which are as culturally normative as possible" (p. 28). Both the means used and the targeted behaviors should be culturally and socially acceptable (Spooner & Brown, 2011). When evaluating the outcomes these individuals are working toward, Wolfensberger (1972) established a criterion of normalization to consider. This criterion provided a means to determine an individual's quality of life through analyzing the individual's (a) normal rhythm of the day, (b) normal rhythm of the week, (c) normal rhythm of the year, (d) normal experiences of the life cycle, (e) normal respect, (f) living in a sexual world, (g) normal economic standards, and (h) normal environmental standards (Spooner & Brown, 2011; Wolfensberger, 1972). The guiding principle of normalization provides a foundation upon

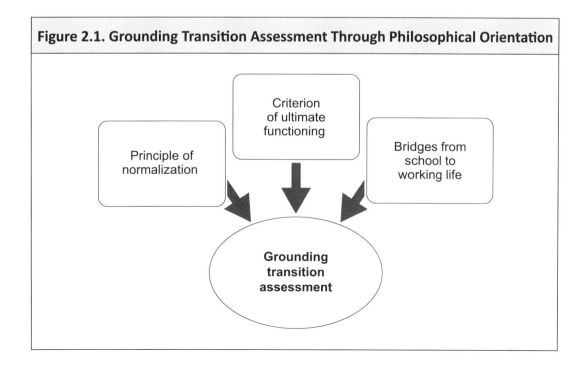

Figure 2.1. Grounding Transition Assessment Through Philosophical Orientation

which to develop an education system that includes and supports individuals meaningfully (Pancsofar & Blackwell, 1986). By declaring the need for integration and charging communities to change, the principle of normalization became a rallying cry advancing the philosophy of improved treatment of individuals with disabilities (Spooner & Brown, 2011; Wolfensberger, 1972).

Criterion of Ultimate Functioning

Using the principle of normalization as its backbone, the criterion of ultimate functioning (Brown et al., 1976) set the stage for promoting "the training of meaningful skills that would increase the likelihood of inclusive placements, and give people skills to function in complex community settings" (Spooner & Brown, 2011, p. 507). The criterion of ultimate functioning challenges educators to teach students skills that generalize to natural environments (i.e., teaching tasks that require real materials in real settings to help assist in real-life problem solving; Brown et al., 1976; Spooner & Brown, 2011). This requires educators to examine the current and future environments of their students with disabilities, determining the most critical skills necessary to survive in a variety of environments (e.g., employment, independent living) and teaching those skills (Brown et al., 1976; Spooner & Brown, 2011). With exposure and acquisition of these skills, there is an enhanced probability of individuals with disabilities living a life that they deem significant and fulfilling (Morningstar, Lee, Lattin, & Murray, 2016).

Bridges From School to Working Life

For students with disabilities, "successful transition ultimately requires employment opportunities" (Will, 1983, p. 8). This statement leads into the final guiding principle, bridges from school to working life (Will, 1983). This principle considers the transition from high school to an employment setting an outcome-oriented process; the transition is a metaphoric bridge that connects the security and structure of high school to adult life, where opportunities and risks take place (Will, 1983). Although experiences and services leading to employment vary among individuals and the communities in which they live, personalized support is vital (Will, 1983). Affording ongoing support to students with disabilities throughout their employment endeavors can cultivate a positive transition experience and help to produce productive citizens (Repetto et al., 2011). With the three guiding principles operating as the foundation used to drive all decisions when working with students with disabilities, the remainder of this chapter will focus on how these guiding principles can be used to inform transition assessment.

The Law Regarding Transition Assessment

In 1990, after reauthorization of the Education for All Handicapped Children Act as the Individuals With Disabilities Education Act, the U.S. Congress mandated that the individualized education program (IEP) team needed to prepare students with disabilities for postsecondary life (Norlin, 2010; Petcu, Yell, Cholewicki, & Plotner, 2014). With this amendment, IEPs were to include a postsecondary transition plan (Prince, Plotner, & Yell, 2014); previously, IEPs focused on goals that were strictly specific to the school setting. Subsequent amendments of IDEA in 1997 and 2004 reinforced this call to action, emphasizing the need to better prepare students for postsecondary life (Petcu et al., 2014; Prince et al., 2014).

The purpose of special education is to provide free and appropriate education and services that meets the needs of students with IEPs and prepare them for postsecondary education, integrated employment, and independent living (Martin & McConnell, 2017). To accomplish this, students' IEPs must include postsecondary goals describing where these students would like to learn, work, and live (Martin & McConnell, 2017). Providing a vehicle for educators, postsecondary goals and related transition services drive the transition planning process, which includes developing meaningful postsecondary goals, annual goals, and coordinated activities based on students' interests and needs mediated by community opportunities (Martin & McConnell, 2017).

During its 2004 authorization, an addendum to IDEA added several transition-related IEP requirements, which included an introduction of the concept of transition assessment. *Transition assessment* is the process of collecting information on students' preferences, interests, needs, and strengths and writing annual goals that will help facilitate attainment of postsecondary goals (Neubert & Leconte, 2013); this is an ongoing process.

IDEA (2006) requires that two or more transition assessments be used annually to identify students' preferences, interests, needs, and strengths to develop the transition section of the IEP (Neubert & Leconte, 2013). The annual nature of this assessment is important, as students can change as they mature—including their potential vocational interests. Prince and colleagues (2014) examined district court findings across the United States involving postsecondary transition planning, and recommended that, for students with IEPs, school teams (a) use multiple transition assessments across transition domains (i.e., education and training, employment, and independent living), (b) use at least one formal transition assessment with supporting validity evidence and not solely rely on informal transition assessments as a part of a comprehensive transition assessment battery, and (c) maximize student participation in the transition planning process.

Types of Transition Assessments

The transition assessment process is ongoing, involving a variety of stakeholders to strategize and administer them (Neubert & Leconte, 2013). When gathered and compiled, the data collected from transition assessments drive both secondary and postsecondary goals in the IEP (Neubert & Leconte, 2013) and displays a student's current preferences, interests, needs, and strengths as they relate to the demands of current and future working, education, living, personal, and social environments (Brown et al., 1976; Sitlington & Payne, 2004).

Transition assessments should answer the following questions (see Brown et al., 1976; Greene, 2003; Will, 1983):

- What skills and strengths does the student currently possess?
- What are the student's preferences relative to postsecondary environments in the areas of education or training, employment, and independent living?
- Within those environments, what are the formal and informal expectations, rules, and standards for behavior?
- What are the essential skills the student needs to learn to facilitate success in the next environment?
- What types of ongoing support will the student need to be successful in the current and preferred future environments?

Educators and other IEP team members need to use a variety of transition assessments to assess a multitude of domains. Two resources for up-to-date assessment information are (a) the National Technical Assistance Center on Transition (NTACT), which publishes the *Age Appropriate Transition Assessment Toolkit* (2016); and (b) the University of Oklahoma's Zarrow Center for Learning Enrichment (www.ou.edu/education/centers-and-partnerships/zarrow.), whose website provides the names of transition assessments and how to obtain them. Transition assessments are organized by outcome domains (i.e., education and training, employment, independent living) and come in two arrangements: formal and informal.

Formal Assessments

Formal transition assessments are standardized instruments for measuring an array of items and include descriptions of their norming process, reliability, validity, recommended use, reading level, and direction for administration (Neubert & Leconte, 2013; NTACT, 2016). In order to appropriately identify students' preferences, interests, needs, and strengths and then develop the transition section of the IEP, teams must use transition assessments with ample validity evidence supporting their use (Martin & McConnell, 2017).

Informal Assessments

In contrast to formal transition assessments, informal transition assessments lack formal norming processes, reliability, and validity information (Neubert & Leconte, 2013). Many states across the country are still in the development stages of establishing policy and providing guidance related to transition assessments (Morningstar & Liss, 2008); thus, there are a limited number of developed for students with significant support needs (Martin & McConnell, 2017). Because of this, many educators use transition assessments that are not well developed or intended for these students and which fail to provide the most basic validity evidence advocating use of their results (Martin & McConnell, 2017). When using informal transition assessments, interpreting results with caution and acknowledging the use and nature of these assessments during transition-planning discussions and IEP meetings is imperative (Martin & McConnell, 2017). (See Table 2.1).

Choice Making and Situational Assessments

Choice making, "the expression of a preference between two or more options" (Shogren & Wehmeyer, 2017, p. 260), has received significant attention in the research literature. Individuals with disabilities have had limited opportunities for choice making, which negatively affects the development of skills related to decision making and self-determination. For example, Wehmeyer and Metzler (1995) found that individuals with disabilities had fewer choice-making opportunities regarding activities such as where they lived and worked, activities in which they wanted to participate during the evenings or weekends, and individuals with whom they wanted to spend time. However, research has shown that when students with disabilities are provided with choice-making opportunities, adaptive behaviors increase while problem behaviors decrease (Shogren, Faggella-Luby, Bae, & Wehmeyer, 2004). When decisions are preference-driven, individuals with disabilities live more fulfilling lives because the choices they make match their interests and are more meaningful to them (Martin, Woods, Sylvester, & Gardner, 2005).

As mentioned earlier, there are a limited number of transition assessments developed for students with significant support needs, and the ones that are available do not effectively measure the transition domains to successfully transition these students from high school to postsecondary life. These assessments measure a single-point-in-time interest or skill, producing a static profile of the student (Martin et al., 2005). For example, interest inventory results often change as students with disabilities gain additional experiences (Martin et al., 2005). Using a repeated measures situational assessment approach provides an evolving and dynamic, rather than a static, profile and provides ample data to ensure a

Table 2.1. Formal and Informal Transition Assessments	
Formal transition assessments	**Informal transition assessments**
• Adaptive Behavior Assessment System, Third Edition (Harrison & Oakland, 2015) • ARC Self-Determination Scale (Wehmeyer, 1995) • Becker Work Adjustment Profile: 2 (Becker, 2005) • Picture Interest Career Survey, Second Edition (Brady, 2011) • Reading-Free Vocational Interest Inventory, Second Edition (Becker, 2000) • Self-Determination Inventory: Student-Report (Shogren, Wehmeyer, & Little, 2017) • Supports Intensity Scale (Thompson et al., 2004) • Transition Assessment and Goal Generator (Martin, Hennessey, McConnell, Terry, & Willis, 2015) • Transition Planning Inventory, Second Edition (Patton & Clark, 2014)	• Brigance Transition Skills Inventory (Curriculum Associates, Inc., 2010) • Casey Life Skills (Casey Family Programs, 2017) • ChoiceMaker Self-Determination Assessment, Third Edition (Martin & Marshall, 2016) • Enderle-Severson Transition Rating Scale-S (Severson, Enderle, & Hoover, 2006) • Job Observation and Behavior Scale (Rosenberg & Brady, 2000) • Personal Preference Indicators (Moss, 2006) • Transition-to-Work Inventory, Third Edition (Liptak, 2012) • Work Personality Profile and Computer Report (Bolton & Neath, 2008)

match between student preferences and work environments. This will ultimately produce more relevant vocational opportunities for the student (Martin, Mithaug, Oliphint, Husch, & Frazier, 2002).

Identified by Lohrmann-O'Rourke and Browder (1998), self-directed assessments can help to determine preferred entry-level employment choices by using a repeated measures situational assessment. Students with disabilities choose (a) employment settings (e.g., construction site, grocery store), (b) activities (e.g., assemble and disassemble, bag items, bring in carts), and (c) characteristics (e.g., quiet, outside, wear a uniform, around many people) associated with employment settings and then compare their choices to employment opportunities existing in their community (Martin et al., 2005). This process is repeated until consistent choices emerge, at which point students are matched to employment opportunities based on their self-identified preferences (Martin et al., 2005). A repeated measures situational assessment can be accomplished through pictures or videos, where (a) students select and study pairs of pictures or watch paired videos illustrating entry-level employment opportunities available in their communities; (b) utilizing an omission procedure, students choose the job they want to do; (c) students experience their job choice in the community; (d) students evaluate their experience; and (e) students make new choices based on their experience and what they learned (Martin et al., 2005). Again, a repeated measures situational assessment provides a student profile that evolves, is dynamic, and is rich with preferred employment choices and possible vocational opportunities. (See Figure 2.2). The process includes multiple steps:

- Create method to determine interests.
- Conduct first round of assessment.
- Conduct repeated rounds of assessment.
- Have the student select interest areas.
- Provide work experience opportunities.
- Collect data to evaluate experiences.
- Summarize assessment results.
- Continue to assess preferences.

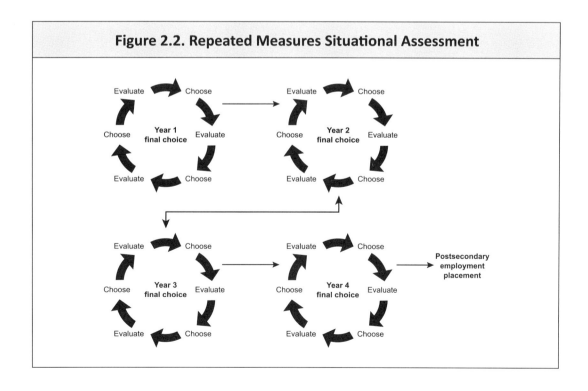

Figure 2.2. Repeated Measures Situational Assessment

CASE STUDY 2.1 (Charlie)

Charlie, a 15-year-old freshman with a developmental disability, has expressed interest in participating in postsecondary employment. To identify his employment interests, his case manager, Mrs. Thompson, developed 16 short video clips of local employment opportunities. Each video depicted an employment setting, activity, and two characteristics of an entry-level job that was readily available in the community. Charlie watched the randomly paired videos and selected the job he liked best from each pair. After the first round of video watching, Mrs. Thompson randomly paired Charlie's first-round choices; he repeated the viewing and choice process, and this continued until Charlie had chosen one employment opportunity. Charlie's top employment choice was prep work at a restaurant including preparing cutlery and filling the napkin dispenser and salt and pepper shakers.

With his confirmed choice, Mrs. Thompson asked Charlie if he would like to watch or participate in the job in the community. Charlie decided to do both, and the school arranged for him to observe and participate at a local restaurant. At the end of the work experience, Mrs. Thompson and Charlie evaluated the employment experience, graphing Charlie's evaluation of his experience.

The process of using a repeated measures situational assessment was repeated throughout the semester, providing Charlie with the opportunity to experience many of his employment interests in his community. Graphing the data for each of his experiences helped Mrs. Thompson identify emerging patterns, which were grounded in the community-based jobs Charlie experienced, and his preferences become clear relative to postsecondary employment options.

At the end of the semester, Charlie's top employment setting and activity choices included restaurant prep work followed by selling candy and popcorn at the movie theater. Charlie's top job characteristics included working inside, working in the afternoon or evening, being with people, and wearing a uniform. As Charlie progressed through high school, he gained further knowledge and experiences. Mrs. Thompson continued conducting the repeated measures situational assessment because she understood that, with his acquisition of new knowledge and experiences, Charlie's employment preferences could change. The repeated measures situational assessment allowed her to measure and evaluate these changes on an ongoing basis. With this information, Mrs. Thompson was able to accurately and effectively individualize and tailor her instruction for Charlie and prepare him for postsecondary employment.

A repeated measures situational assessment process offers individuals with disabilities multiple opportunities to make a real choice and act upon that choice by watching or trying chosen community jobs (Martin et al., 2005). The process facilitates the awareness of community-based jobs for students who have had little to no work experience, and affords them the opportunity to explore their interests (Martin et al., 2005). Students with disabilities can make informed and clear employment choices when afforded the opportunity. The repeated measures situational assessment process can help to promote the advocacy and decision-making skills of students with disabilities and provide insights to preferred job choices and work environments (Martin et al., 2005).

Summary

Transition assessment is a fundamental component of transition planning for students with disabilities. Data from transition assessments support educators in determining the appropriate course of study during high school, the transition pathway to postsecondary settings, and the level of success the student is achieving in the current course of study relative to their pursuit of postsecondary endeavors. As an ongoing process, transition assessment collects data on the preferences, interests, needs, and strengths relative to postsecondary environments in the areas of education, employment, and independent living.

This chapter introduced three approaches to transition assessment: (a) formal transition assessment, (b) informal transition assessment, and (c) repeated measures situational assessment. These strategies are effective in meeting IDEA legislative requirements and providing students with disabilities the opportunity to further explore their own postsecondary goals. Without the utilization of these three types of transition assessments for students with disabilities to develop and drive the transition planning process, positive outcomes in postsecondary education, employment, and independent living may not take place as intended by IDEA legislation. As reported by Newman, Wagner, Cameto, and Knokey (2009), adults with disabilities are twice as likely to be fired or laid off from their jobs as their same-aged peers. Therefore, transition assessments are extremely important to match student preferences to postsecondary environments. Regardless of the type utilized, transition assessment should take place in real-world contexts. With the use of the practices described in this chapter with fidelity, students with disabilities will gain valuable experience that will prove helpful in their positive success—both in school and beyond.

References

Becker, R. L. (2000). *Reading-Free Vocational Interest Inventory: 2*. Columbus, OH: Elbern.

Becker, R. L. (2005). *Becker Work Adjustment Profile: 2*. Columbus, OH: Elbern.

Bolton, B., & Neath, J. (2008). *Work personality profile and computer report*. Austin, TX: PRO-ED.

Brady, R. P, (2011). *Picture Interest Career Survey, Second Edition*. St. Paul, MN: JIST/EMC Publishing.

Brown, L., Nietupski, J., & Hamre-Nietupski, S. (1976). Criterion of ultimate functioning. In M. A. Thomas (Ed.), *Hey, don't forget about me! Education's investment in the severely, profoundly, and multiply handicapped* (pp. 2–15). Reston, VA: Council for Exceptional Children.

Casey Family Programs. (2017). *Casey Life Skills*. Seattle, WA: Author.

Curriculum Associates, Inc. (2010). *Brigance Transition Skills Inventory*. North Billerica, MA: Author.

Funk, R. A. (1987). Disability rights: From class to caste in the contest of civil rights. In A. Gartner & T. Joe (Eds.), *Images of the disabled: Disabling images* (pp. 7–30. New York, NY: Praeger.

Greene, G. (2003). Transition assessment. In G. Greene & C. A. Kochhar-Bryant (Eds.), *Pathways to successful transition for youth with disabilities* (pp. 230–253). Upper Saddle River, NJ: Merrill Prentice Hall.

Harrison, P., & Oakland, T. (2015). *Adaptive Behavior Assessment System, Third Edition*. Torrance, CA: Western Psychological Services.

Individuals With Disabilities Education Act, 20 U.S.C. §§ 1400 *et seq*. (2006 & Supp. V. 2011)

Liptak, J. J. (2012). *Transition-to-Work Inventory, Third Edition*. St. Paul, MN: JIST/EMC Publishing.

Lohrmann-O'Rourke, S., & Browder, D. M. (1998). Empirically based methods to assess the preferences of individuals with severe disabilities. *American Journal on Mental Retardation, 103*, 146–161. doi:10.1352/0895-8017(1998)103<0146:EBMTAT>2.0.CO;2

Martin, J., Hennessey, M., McConnell, A., Terry, R., & Willis, D. (2015). *Transition Assessment & Goal Generator*. Norman, OK: University of Oklahoma Zarrow Center for Learning Enrichment.

Martin, J. E., & Marshall, L. H. (2016). *ChoiceMaker Self-Determination Assessment—Third Edition*. Norman, OK: University of Oklahoma Zarrow Center for Learning Enrichment.

Martin, J. E., & McConnell, A. E. (2017). Transition planning. In M. L. Wehmeyer & K. A. Shogren (Eds.), *Handbook of research-based practices for educating students with intellectual disability* (pp. 151–166). New York, NY: Routledge.

Martin, J. E., Mithaug, D. E., Oliphint, J. H., Husch, J. V., & Frazier, E. S. (2002). *Self-directed employment: A handbook for transition teachers and employment specialists*. Baltimore, MD: Paul H. Brookes.

Martin, J. E., Woods, L. L., Sylvester, L., & Gardner, J. E. (2005). A challenge to self-determination: Disagreement between the vocational choices made by individuals with severe disabilities and their caregivers. *Research & Practice for Persons with Severe Disabilities, 30*, 147–153. doi:10.2511/rpsd.30.3.147

Morningstar, M. E., Lee, H., Lattin, D. L., & Murray, A. K. (2016). An evaluation of the technical adequacy of a revised measure of quality indicators of transition. *Career Development and Transition for Exceptional Individuals, 39*, 227–236. doi:10.1177/2165143415589925

Morningstar, M. E., & Liss, J. M. (2008). A preliminary investigation of how states are responding to the TA requirements under IDEIA 2004. *Career Development for Exceptional Individuals, 31*, 48–55. doi:10.1177/0885728807313776

Moss, J. (2006). *Personal Preference Indicators*. Oklahoma City: University of Oklahoma Health Sciences Center.

National Technical Assistance Center on Transition (NTACT). (2016). *Age appropriate transition assessment toolkit* (4th ed.). Charlotte, NC: Author.

Neubert, D. A., & Leconte, P. J. (2013). Age-appropriate transition assessment: The position of the division on career development and transition. *Career Development and Transition for Exceptional Individuals, 36*, 72–83. doi:10.1177/2165143413487768

Newman, L., Wagner, M., Cameto, R., & Knokey, A. M. (2009). *The post-high school outcomes of youth with disabilities up to 4 years after high school: A report from the National Longitudinal Transition Study-2 (NLTS-2)* (NCSER 2009-3017). Menlo Park, CA: SRI International.

Norlin, J. W. (2010). *Postsecondary transition services: An IDEA compliance guide for IEP teams*. Palm Beach Gardens, FL: LRP.

Pancsofar, E., & Blackwell, R. (1986). *A user's guide to community entry for the severely handicapped*. Albany, NY: State University of New York Press.

Patton, J. R., & Clark, G. M. (2014). *Transition Planning Inventory, Second Edition*. Austin, TX: PRO-ED.

Petcu, S. D., Yell, M. L., Cholewicki, J. M., & Plotner, A. J. (2014). Issues and policy and law in transition services: Implications for special education leaders. *Journal of Special Education Leadership, 27*, 66–75.

Prince, A. M. T., Plotner, A. J., & Yell, M. J. (2014). Postsecondary transition and the courts: An update. *Journal of Disability Policy Studies, 25*, 41–47. doi:10.1177/1044207314530469

Repetto, J. B., McGorray, S. P., Wang, H., Podmostko, M., Andrews, W. D., Lubbers, J., & Gritz, S. (2011). The high school experience: What students with and without disabilities report as the leave school. *Career Development and Transition for Exceptional Individuals, 34*, 142–152. doi:10.1177/0885728811414699

Rosenberg, H., & Brady, M. (2000). *Job Observation and Behavior Scale*. Wood Dale, IL: Stoelting.

Severson, S., Enderle, J., & Hoover, J. (2006). *Enderle-Severson Transition Rating Scale–S*. Columbus, OH: ESTR.

Shogren, K. A., Faggella-Luby, M., Bae, S. J., & Wehmeyer, M. L. (2004). The effect of choice-making as an intervention for problem behavior: A meta-analysis. *Journal of Positive Behavior Interventions, 6*, 228–237. doi:10.1177/10983007040060040401

Shogren, K. A., & Wehmeyer, M. L. (2017). Self-determination and goal attainment. In M. L. Wehmeyer & K. A. Shogren (Eds.), *Handbook of research-based practices for educating students with intellectual disability* (pp. 151–166). New York, NY: Routledge.

Shogren, K. A., Wehmeyer, M. L., & Little, T. J. (2017). *Self-Determination Inventory: Student Report*. Lawrence: Kansas University Center on Developmental Disabilities.

Sitlington, P. L., & Payne, E. M. (2004). Information needed for postsecondary education: Can we provide it as part of the transition assessment process? *Learning Disabilities: A Contemporary Journal, 2*, 1–14.

Spooner, F., & Brown, F. (2011). Educating students with significant cognitive disabilities. In J. M. Kauffman & D. P. Hallahan (Eds.), *Handbook of special education* (pp. 503–515). New York, NY: Routledge.

Thompson, J. R., Bryant, B. L., Campbell, E. M., Craig, E. M., Hughes, C. M., Rotholz, D. A., ... Wehmeyer, M. L. (2004). *Support Intensity Scale*. Washington, DC: American Association on Intellectual and Developmental Disabilities.

Ward, M. J. (1988). The many facets of self-determination. *National Information Center for Children and Youth with Handicaps Transition Summary, 5*, 2–3.

Webster, Q. (n.d.). *The need to preserve movable cultural historical heritage*. Retrieved from http://155.187.2.69/heritage/strategy/pubs/003culturalheritagepreservationfoundation.pdf

Wehmeyer, M. L. (1995). *ARC Self-Determination Scale*. Washington, DC: The Arc of the United States.

Wehmeyer, M. L., & Metzler, C. A. (1995). How self-determined are people with mental retardation? The National Consumer Survey. *Mental Retardation, 33*, 111–119.

Will, M. (1983). *OSERS programming for the transition of youth with disabilities: Bridges from school to working life*. Washington, DC: Office of Special Education and Rehabilitative Services. Retrieved from https://files.eric.ed.gov/fulltext/ED256132.pdf

Wolfensberger, W. (1972). *Normalization: The principle of normalization in human services*. Toronto, Canada: National Institute on Mental Retardation.

CHAPTER 3
Transition-Focused Program Plans
Kathryn M. Burke, Karrie A. Shogren, and Michael L. Wehmeyer

Objectives:
- Identify key components of program plans for transition-age students.
- Describe evidence-based practices for transition planning.
- Describe the importance of student involvement and self-determination in transition planning.

Chapter 3 introduces the topic of transition-focused program plans, and how these plans can be used to support youth with developmental disabilities, including those with autism spectrum disorder and intellectual disability, as they transition from school to the adult world. The transition from school to the adult world is an exciting, complex, and potentially overwhelming experience for a young person. Although students with disabilities move from school to adulthood just like their peers, they often need unique services and supports during this time. The key to providing those supports and services lies in comprehensive, thoughtful planning. This chapter takes a closer look at transition planning and introduces evidence-based strategies that effectively enhance the process.

Key Terminology	
Individualized plan for employment	A written document that identifies a chosen employment outcome for an individual and the specific vocational rehabilitation services to achieve that outcome. The IPE also indicates who will provide the vocational rehabilitation services and the criteria to evaluate progress toward the employment outcome, as well as information on supported employment and post-employment services (if determined appropriate or necessary; see 29 U.S.C. § 722[b][3].)

Key Terminology (cont'd)	
Individualized service plan	A plan of services and supports for a person with disabilities transitioning to adult services. Team members incorporate the person's preferences, interests, needs, and strengths (commonly through person-centered planning; Mazzotti, Kelley, & Coco, 2015) to create goals, objectives, and a plan for services (U.S. Department of Education, 2017).
Interagency collaboration	A "clear, purposeful, and carefully designed process that promotes cross agency, cross program, and cross disciplinary collaborative efforts leading to tangible transition outcomes for youth" (Rowe et al., 2014, p. 10).

The Individuals With Disabilities Education Act (IDEA, 2006) requires that all students with an individualized education program (IEP) ages 16 and older receive services that enable their transition from school to adult life. Transition services are also addressed in Section 504 of the Rehabilitation Act of 1973, as amended by the Workforce Innovation and Opportunity Act (WIOA, 2009), which authorizes pre-employment transition services, transition services, job placement services, other vocational rehabilitation services, and supported employment for young people with disabilities.

Transition Planning

The transition from high school to adult roles and the responsibilities intrinsic to adult life represents a significant change for all students as they explore postsecondary education, integrated employment, and independent community living. To support students with disabilities during this significant time period, transition services must be addressed in the first IEP that will be in effect when a student is 16 years old, although planning may begin earlier. IEP teams—which include the students—are tasked with identifying appropriate courses of study, experiences, and supports that will assist students in achieving their postsecondary goals. In addition, IEP teams continue to plan and address the students' other annual IEP goals even as transition services are added.

In planning for the transition from school to employment, an **individualized plan for employment** can be developed and approved by the time the student leaves the school setting to document the provision of services and supports needed to achieve employment outcomes as the student transitions beyond the classroom. An **individualized service plan** can also be developed to address services and supports in other aspects of life (e.g., community living and participation) as the third component of a transition-focused program plan. Because creating meaningful, inclusive transition-focused program plans requires teamwork, the importance of interagency collaboration is paramount.

The value of interagency collaboration is evident from the extensive literature on its influence on postschool outcomes (Test, Mazzotti, et al., 2009) and successful methods of implementation (Johnson, Zorn, Tam, Lamontagne, & Johnson, 2003; Noonan, Morningstar, & Gaumer, 2008). Transition services involve a collaborative effort by students, their families, state education agencies, local education agencies, adult service providers, and state vocational rehabilitation agencies. The school is responsible for bringing in representatives from outside agencies (e.g., vocational rehabilitation)—with the consent of family members or the student (if at the age of majority)—as a part of the transition planning team. State and local education agencies, adult service providers, and agencies such as vocational rehabilitation can develop formal **interagency agreements** to address the system of transition services, and work together to implement the provisions of the agreement and support students in achieving their postschool goals.

Predictors of Postschool Outcomes

Researchers began documenting poor postschool outcomes for young people with disabilities beginning in the late 1980s and 1990s (e.g., Blackorby & Wagner, 1996; Hasazi, Gordon, & Roe, 1985). There has been some improvement in transition outcomes for youth with disabilities, but their postschool outcomes continue to lag behind those of their peers (Wagner, Newman, Cameto, Levine, & Garza, 2006). Given the increased awareness of this issue, transition education and services have received greater focus (Kohler & Field, 2003).

In an effort to identify why some young adults with disabilities thrive in the real world while others flounder, researchers have worked to identify predictive factors of postschool outcomes. Benz, Lindstrom, and Yovanoff (2000) found career-related work experience and completion of student-related transition goals to be highly associated with improved graduation and employment outcomes. More recently, Test, Mazzotti, and colleagues (2009) examined the literature on secondary transition and identified 16 evidence-based, in-school predictors of postschool outcomes in the areas of education, employment, and independent community living for students with disabilities. These predictors were further defined in 2014 (Rowe et al.). Each of the identified predictors is listed and described in Table 3.1, along with the associated outcome area and level of evidence. These findings demonstrate a set of research-based predictors of postschool success based on quality correlational research. The question for IEP teams is how these predictors of positive postschool outcomes can be put into practice through transition planning.

Table 3.1. Predictors of Positive Postschool Outcomes

Evidence-based predictor[a]	Definition[b]	Outcome area and level of evidence[a]		
		Education	Employment	Independent living
Career awareness	Students learn about career options to find a fit that matches their preferences, interests, needs, strengths, and goals.	Potential	Potential	Not established
Community experiences	Students participate in community-based activities outside the school setting while also receiving educational and vocational instruction and support.	Not established	Potential	Not established
Exit exam requirements/ high school diploma status	Students take standardized state tests to show proficiency to earn a high school diploma and meet exit exam requirements. Students earn a high school diploma after meeting state requirements such as completing core coursework.	Not established	Potential	Not established
Inclusion in general education	Students participate in the general education curriculum and in general education settings alongside peers with and without disabilities.	Moderate	Moderate	Moderate
Interagency collaboration	Professionals across agencies, programs, and disciplines work together in an intentional way to support transition outcomes for students.	Potential	Potential	Not established
Occupational courses	Students take courses to gain a better understanding of career options and develop skill sets and experiences related to selected jobs.	Potential	Potential	Not established

Table 3.1. Predictors of Positive Postschool Outcomes (cont'd)					
Evidence-based predictor[a]	**Definition**[b]	Outcome area and level of evidence[a]		
		Education	Employment	Independent living
Paid employment/ work experience	Students participate in real-world jobs, either for pay, as an internship, or as a training or shadowing experience.	Moderate	Moderate	Moderate
Parental involvement	Students' families participate in the transition planning process as informed, active team members.	Not established	Potential	Not established
Program of study	Students take a personalized series of classes and community and work experiences to prepare for postschool life.	Not established	Potential	Not established
Self-advocacy/self-determination	Students engage in actions to set and attain goals, and use skills like choice making, problem solving, and self-regulation.	Potential	Potential	Not established
Self-care/ independent living skills	Students are prepared to manage personal care and community living with the necessary social skills, money management skills, and health and wellness skills.	Potential	Potential	Moderate
Social skills	Students have the necessary skills to communicate and interact appropriately with others, such as oral and written communication, speaking and listening, and responding to social problems.	Potential	Potential	Not established
Support system	Students have family, friends, and professionals to help them meet their individual transition and postschool goals.	Potential	Potential	Potential

Table 3.1. Predictors of Positive Postschool Outcomes (cont'd)

Evidence-based predictor[a]	Definition[b]	Outcome area and level of evidence[a]		
		Education	Employment	Independent living
Transition program	Students participate in a designated set of courses, experiences, and planning to prepare for desired outcomes in postschool life.	Moderate	Potential	Not established
Vocational education	Students take a series of classes to develop skills for selected careers.	Moderate	Moderate	Not established
Work study	Students receive instruction and work experience as a combined academic and vocational approach to job preparation.	Not established	Moderate	Not established

Note. Potential level of evidence must include: "(a) one a priori (i.e., planned hypothesis prior to analysis) study and/or (b) two or more exploratory (no specific hypothesis) studies with significant correlations between predictor and outcome variables" (Test, Mazzotti, et al., 2009, p. 164). Moderate level of evidence must include: "(a) two a priori (i.e., planned hypothesis prior to analysis) studies with consistent significant correlations between predictor and outcome variables ... and (b) effect size calculations or data to calculate effect size" (p. 164).
[a]Test, Mazzotti, et al., 2009. [b]Rowe et al., 2014.

The National Secondary Transition Technical Assistance Center (NTACT) has identified some evidence-based practices as predictors of postschool success for students with disabilities (Test, Mazzotti, et al., 2009). These strategies include:

- Collaborating across state and local agencies
- Involving students
- Promoting self-determination skills
- Providing employment opportunities
- Planning transition to adulthood

There are specific strategies for each predictor, which educators can use with students.

Collaboration at State and Local Levels

The factors of successful partnerships include (a) commitment, (b) communication, (c) strong leadership, (d) understanding the culture of collaborating agencies,

(e) engaging in preplanning, (f) providing adequate resources for collaboration, and (g) minimizing defensive or protective behaviors by collaborating agencies (Johnson et al., 2003). Interagency collaboration is the linchpin of transition planning. In a study focusing on facilitating interagency collaboration through effective case management, Balcazar and colleagues (2012) found enhanced employment outcomes for transition-age minority youth with disabilities. A variety of resources are available to facilitate strong interagency collaboration, including 11 key strategies used by high-performing local education agencies (see Figure 3.1; Noonan et al., 2008).

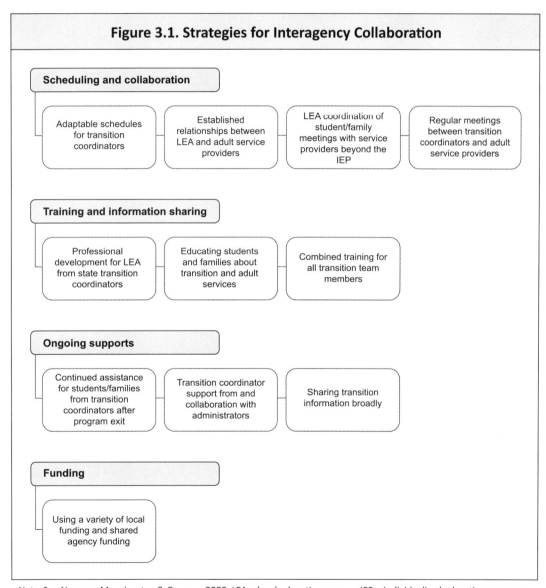

Note. See Noonan, Morningstar, & Gaumer, 2008. LEA = local education agency; IEP = individualized education program.

Student Involvement

Student participation in transition planning is strongly linked to postschool success (Halpern, Yovanoff, Doren, & Benz, 1995; Wei, Wagner, Hudson, Yu, & Javitz, 2016), but students too rarely have opportunities to take leadership roles in transition planning (Shogren & Plotner, 2012). Students have reported not knowing the reasons for IEP meetings or what to do at the meeting (Martin, Marshall, & Sale, 2004). The self-directed IEP is one evidence-based practice for increasing student participation in IEP meetings (Martin, Van Dycke, Christensen, Gardner, & Lovett, 2006). Through a multimedia lesson package, students learn to actively participate in and lead their own IEP meetings. Other evidence-based practices include the *Whose Future Is It Anyway?* curriculum (Wehmeyer, Palmer, Lee, Williams-Diehm, & Shogren, 2011) and student-directed transition planning (Woods, Sylvester, & Martin, 2010).

CASE STUDY 3.1 (Maria)

Maria is a 17-year-old student with intellectual disability who enjoys participating in her school's art club, going to movies with her friends, and sharing photos with friends and family on social media. Based on her interests in art, the vocational rehabilitation counselor on her IEP team helped Maria obtain an internship at an art gallery in town, where she helps to sort inventory. Maria enjoys working and learning at the art gallery, but she has also expressed interest in getting a paid job. Maria's internship is an important predictor of postschool success; however, her transition-focused program plan could be improved by incorporating more evidence-based predictors of postschool outcomes.

Maria's case manager is aware that it is part of her role to support her students and their families in connecting with local service agencies and ensuring that services are actually received. She also recognizes the need to incorporate more preplanning into the team's efforts, which has not begun exploring options and setting goals for where Maria would like to live as an adult.

Skills Associated With Self-Determination

Self-determination is "acting as the causal agent in one's life. Self-determined people (i.e., causal agents) act in service to freely chosen goals. Self-determined actions function to enable a person to be the causal agent in his or her life" (Shogren et al., 2015). Choice making, decision making, problem solving, goal setting and attainment, self-management, self-advocacy, self-awareness, and self-knowledge are all skills associated with self-determination (Shogren, 2013). By teaching students these skills and creating opportunities for students to apply them, causal agency and self-determination develop.

Although self-determination has been found to predict postschool employment outcomes for young adults with disabilities (Shogren et al., 2015), parents have reported limited opportunities for their transition-age children to learn these skills (Carter et al., 2013; Shogren, 2012). Given this discrepancy, the promotion of self-determination is essential for transition-age youth. Educators can use the *Self-Determined Learning Model of Instruction* (SDLMI; Shogren, Wehmeyer, Burke, & Palmer, 2017) to empower students to self-regulate and practice problem solving in order to set and attain goals and enhance their self-determination.

CASE STUDY 3.2 (Maria, cont'd)

*Maria began to work on enhancing her goal-setting and problem-solving skills in a number of ways. Using the **Self-Determined Learning Model of Instruction** with the support of her case manager, Maria set a goal of showcasing paintings at her school's art exhibit. Based on her desire to seek paid employment, the vocational rehabilitation service provider found her an opportunity to apply for a paid position at the art store in town. Maria was faced with the choice of continuing her internship at the art gallery or taking a paid position at the art store. The team supported Maria in considering the pros and cons of each option, and she decided to take the paid job at the art store. Given the association between paid work experiences and postschool work status, Maria's choice to leave her internship at the art gallery to begin a paid position will likely benefit her in the future.*

Maria's team also decided to include extended transition services as an element of her individualized service plan. Providing her with vocational assessment and training, job interview preparation, and job coaching would help ease the contrast between in-school supports and adult services.

Employment Opportunities

According to the National Collaborative on Workforce and Disability for Youth (NCWD), paid or unpaid work experiences help students acquire jobs at higher rates postschool, including competitive integrated employment (2011). *Competitive integrated employment* is defined as earning a salary comparable to peers without disabilities and working alongside people with and without disabilities. Carter, Austin, and Trainor (2012) examined predictors of postschool employment success for students with severe disabilities and highlighted a strong association between paid work experiences and postschool work status.

Transition to Adult Services

The transition from the educational system to the adult services system can be relatively seamless if planned appropriately. Structuring the transition program plan to extend services beyond secondary school has support in the literature (Izzo, Cartledge, Miller, Growicki, & Rutkowski, 2000; Test, Fowler, et al., 2009). Youth who received extended transition services—such as vocational assessment and training, job interview preparation, and job coaching—were found to earn significantly higher salaries for 2 years after the termination of services. Incorporating members of adult service agencies into the IEP team during transition planning is an essential component of transition planning, and IEP teams should consider the addition of representatives from service agencies for individuals with disabilities, independent living centers, and the Social Security Administration.

Summary

With thoughtful planning and collaboration, the transition from school to the adult world can be a smooth one. The wealth of literature on evidence-based practices for transition planning offers strategies and resources for successful instruction and supports. This chapter has highlighted utilizing interagency collaboration to plan employment and transition to adulthood with student involvement and the importance of self-determination skills. With the support of a team, students can receive the right supports to build skill sets, explore opportunities, and set and achieve goals for a meaningful postschool life.

References

Balcazar, F. E., Taylor-Ritzler, T., Dimpfl, S., Portillo-Pena, N., Guzman, A., Schiff, R., & Murvay, M. (2012). Improving the transition outcomes of low-income minority youth with disabilities. *Exceptionality, 20*, 114–132. doi:10.1080/09362835.2012.670599

Benz, M. R., Lindstrom, L., & Yovanoff, P. (2000). Improving graduation and employment outcomes of students with disabilities: Predictive factors and student perspectives. *Exceptional Children, 66*, 509–529. doi:10.1177/001440290006600405

Blackorby, J., & Wagner, M. (1996). Longitudinal postschool outcomes of youth with disabilities: Findings from the National Longitudinal Transition Study. *Exceptional Children, 62*, 399–413. doi:10.1177/001440299606200502

Carter, E. W., Austin, D., & Trainor, A. A. (2012). Predictors of postschool employment outcomes for young adults with severe disabilities. *Journal of Disability Policy Studies, 23*, 50–63. doi:10.1177/1044207311414680

Carter, E. W., Lane, K. L., Cooney, M., Weir, K., Moss, C. K., & Machalicek, W. (2013). Self-determination among transition-age youth with autism or intellectual disability: Parent perspectives. *Research and Practice for Persons with Severe Disabilities, 38*, 129–138. doi:10.1177/154079691303800301

Halpern, A. S., Yovanoff, P., Doren, B., & Benz, M. R. (1995). Predicting participation in postsecondary education for school leavers with disabilities. *Exceptional Children, 62*, 151–164. doi:10.1177/001440299506200205

Hasazi, S. B., Gordon, L. R., & Roe, C. A. (1985). Factors associated with the employment status of handicapped youth exiting high school from 1979 to 1983. *Exceptional Children, 51*, 455–469. doi:10.1177/001440298505100601

Individuals With Disabilities Education Act, 20 U.S.C. §§ 1400 *et seq*. (2006 & Supp. V. 2011)

Izzo, M. V., Cartledge, G., Miller, L., Growicki, B., & Rutkowski, S. (2000). Increasing employment earnings: Extended transition services that make a difference. *Career Development for Exceptional Individuals, 23*, 139–156. doi:10.1177/088572880002300203

Johnson, L. J., Zorn, D., Tam, B. K., Lamontagne, M., & Johnson, S. A. (2003). Stakeholders' views of factors that impact successful interagency collaboration. *Exceptional Children, 69*, 195–209. doi:10.1177/001440290306900205

Kohler, P., & Field, S. (2003). Transition-focused education: Foundation for the future. *The Journal of Special Education, 37*, 174–183. doi:10.1177/00224669030370030701

Martin, J. E., Marshall, L. H., & Sale, P. (2004). A 3-year study of middle, junior high, and high school IEP meetings. *Exceptional Children, 70*, 285–297. doi:10.1177/001440290407000302

Martin, J. E., Van Dycke, J. L., Christensen, W. R., Gardner, J. E., & Lovett, D. L. (2006). Increasing student participation in IEP meetings: Establishing the self-directed IEP as an evidence-based practice. *Exceptional Children, 72*, 299–316. doi:10.1177/001440290607200303

Mazzotti, V. L., Kelley, K. R., & Coco, C. M. (2015). Effects of self-directed summary of performance on postsecondary education students' participation in person-centered planning meetings. *The Journal of Special Education, 48*, 243–255. doi:10.1177/0022466913483575

National Collaborative on Workforce and Disability for Youth. (2011). *Engaging youth in work experiences: An innovative strategies practice brief*. Washington, DC: Author.

Noonan, P. M., Morningstar, M. E., & Gaumer, A. (2008). Improving interagency collaboration: Effective strategies used by high-performing local districts and communities. *Career Development and Transition for Exceptional Individuals, 31*, 132–143. doi:10.1177/0885728808327149

Rehabilitation Act of 1973, as amended by Pub. L. No. 110-325, to be codified at 29 U.S.C. § 701 (2009).

Rowe, D. A., Alverson, C. Y., Unruh, D., Fowler, C., Kellems, R., & Test, D. W. (2014). A Delphi study to operationalize evidence-based predictors in secondary transition. *Career Development for Exceptional Individuals, 38*, 113–126. doi:10.1177/2165143414526429

Shogren, K. A. (2012). Hispanic mothers' perceptions of self-determination. *Research and Practice for Persons with Severe Disabilities, 37*, 170–184. doi:10.2511/027494812804153561

Shogren, K. A. (2013). *Self-determination and transition planning*. Baltimore, MD: Paul H. Brookes.

Shogren, K. A., & Plotner, A. J. (2012). Transition planning for students with intellectual disability, autism, or other disabilities: Data from the National Longitudinal Transition Study-2. *Intellectual and Developmental Disabilities, 50*, 16–30. doi:10.1352/1934-9556-50.1.16

Shogren, K. A., Wehmeyer, M. L., Burke, K. M., & Palmer, S. B. (2017). *The Self-Determined Learning Model of Instruction: Teacher's guide*. Lawrence, KS: Kansas University Center on Developmental Disabilities.

Shogren, K. A., Wehmeyer, M. L., Palmer, S. B., Forber-Pratt, A. J., Little, T. J., & Lopez, S. (2015). Causal agency theory: Reconceptualizing a functional model of self-determination. *Education and Training in Autism and Developmental Disabilities, 50*, 251–263.

Test, D., Mazzotti, V., Mustian, A., Fowler, C., Kortering, L., & Kohler, P. (2009). Evidence-based secondary transition predictors for improving postschool outcomes for students with disabilities. *Career Development for Exceptional Individuals, 32*, 160–181. doi:10.1177/0885728809346960

Test, D. W., Fowler, C. H., Richter, S. M., White, J., Mazzotti, V., Walker, A. R., … Kortering, L. (2009). Evidence-based practices in secondary transition. *Career Development for Exceptional Individuals, 32*, 115–128. doi:10.1177/0885728809336859

U.S. Department of Education, Office of Special Education and Rehabilitative Services (2017). *A transition guide to postsecondary education and employment for students and youth with disabilities*. Washington, DC: Author. Retrieved from https://www2.ed.gov/about/offices/list/osers/transition/products/postsecondary-transition-guide-2017.pdf

Wagner, M., Newman, L., Cameto, R., Levine, P., & Garza, N. (2006). *An overview of findings from wave 2 of the National Longitudinal Transition Study-2 (NLTS2)* (NCSER 2006–3004). Menlo Park, CA: SRI International.

Wehmeyer, M. L., Palmer, S. B., Lee, Y., Williams-Diehm, K., & Shogren, K. A. (2011). A randomized-trial evaluation of the effect of Whose Future Is It Anyway? on self-determination. *Career Development for Exceptional Individuals, 34*, 45–56. doi:10.1177/0885728810383559

Wei, X., Wagner, M., Hudson, L., Yu, J. W., & Javitz, H. (2016). The effect of transition planning participation and goal-setting on college enrollment among youth with autism spectrum disorders. *Remedial and Special Education, 37*, 3–14. doi:10.1177/0741932515581495

Woods, L. L., Sylvester, L., & Martin, J. E. (2010). Student-directed transition planning: Increasing student knowledge and self-efficacy in the transition planning process. *Career Development for Exceptional Individuals, 33*, 106–114. doi:10.1177/0885728810368056

CHAPTER 4

Person-Centered Planning, Summary of Performance, and Guardianship

L. Lynn Stansberry Brusnahan, Shannon L. Sparks, Debra L. Cote, and Terri Vandercook

Objectives:
- Define the concept of person-centered planning.
- Describe the development and use of the Summary of Performance.
- Review guardianship options.
- Highlight the benefits and effective implementation of person-centered planning, Summary of Performance , and guardianship practices to meet the needs of individuals with disabilities.

This chapter provides an introduction to the topics of person-centered planning, the Summary of Performance, and guardianship as they relate to youth with developmental disabilities, including those with autism spectrum disorder and intellectual disability. Educators and others play a key role in these practices and the successful transition from high school to adult functioning for individuals with disabilities. Thus, this chapter provides information illustrating the essential elements of these three practices.

Key Terminology	
Guardianship	The legal process where a person or company petitions the court to be assigned to make decisions on behalf of a person who is perceived incapable to do so (see Jameson et al., 2015; Millar, 2014; Quality Trust for Individuals With Disabilities, 2014).

Key Terminology (cont'd)	
Person-centered planning	An individualized process that involves supporting a person to define a "high quality of life" and building a partnership between the person who is supported and those who provide support in order to bring purpose and meaning to life (see Timmons, Freeman, Olson, Benway, & Gulaid, 2016).
Person-centered practice	The alignment of service resources and natural supports that gives a person access to the full benefit of community living and ensures receipt of services in a way that supports achieving individual goals.
Person-centered thinking	A mindset that helps to establish the means for a person to live a life that he or she and the people who care about them have good reasons to value.
Summary of Performance	A secondary school exit document based on a student's individual needs and postsecondary goals that is prepared when special education eligibility is terminated due to the student exceeding the state's age eligibility for special education or graduating with a high school diploma.

Educating students and their families about person-centered planning, the Summary of Performance, and guardianship as part of transition programming is important; families of students with disabilities report needing more information and support from educators to facilitate successful postsecondary transitions (Griffin, McMillan, & Hodapp, 2010). *Success* in students' postsecondary transition is defined by both the practices and process that is used to support students and the outcomes of the transition—and all of these are inextricably intertwined.

Person-Centered Planning

Person-centered planning (PCP) is an individualized process that supports individuals with disabilities to identify what they define as a high quality of life and to create a plan for how to bring that purpose and meaning to life (Timmons, Freeman, Olson, Benway, & Gulaid, 2016). This process requires person-centered thinking, which means thinking about how to help establish the means for a person to live a life that he or she values. A support team implements person-centered practice by aligning service resources and natural supports that give individuals with disabilities access to the full benefits of community living and ensure they receive services in a way that helps them achieve individual goals. PCP involves the consideration of all of the transition domains: employment, recreation and leisure, home, community participation, and postsecondary training and education opportunities. Simply put, PCP supports the individual with a disability to:

- Consider his or her goals for the future.
- Make choices from an array of options.
- Achieve personally defined outcomes in the most integrated community setting.
- Receive services in a manner that reflects personal preferences and choices.
- Lead a happy and fulfilled life in places and with people of his or her own choosing.
- Have control over the life he or she wants and has chosen.

Essential Elements of Person-Centered Planning

In the PCP process, the individual's preferences are front and center and this person is listened to and supported by others to pursue desired outcomes for life. The transition plan should not be based on available "programs," but instead based on the person's preferences, interests, needs, and strengths. This plan should include paid and natural supports (e.g., "front door first" approach) that can be put in place to support success. The task of the support team is to help the person plan for the future, not for others to do the planning. In addition to identifying preferences, it may be equally important to identify what the person would find *undesirable* in terms of living, working, playing, and connecting in the community.

There are numerous resources available to provide the structure and guidelines for how to specifically engage in the PCP process, including the Making Action Plans (MAPS) process (see New Jersey Coalition for Inclusive Education, 2013), PATH (Pearpoint, O'Brien, & Forest, 1993), *Whose Future Is It Anyway?* (Wehmeyer, Lawrence, Kelchner, Palmer, Garner, & Soukup, 2004), and *It's My Future!* (Bolding, Wehmeyer, & Lawrence, 2010). Thompson and colleagues (2017) created a guide for planning teams to use PCP with the Supports Intensity Scale—Adult Version (Thompson et al., 2015) assessment. When choosing an approach, ensure that it includes a commitment to quality of life. Although the different approaches create plans that vary in specificity, each creates a personal profile that describes the person for whom the plan is being created. This profile

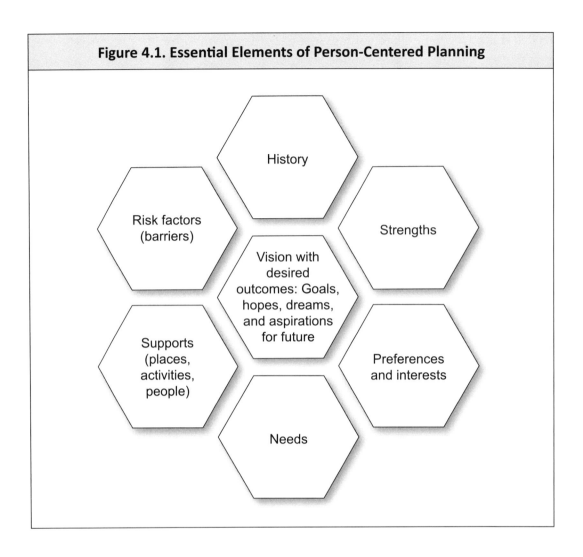

Figure 4.1. Essential Elements of Person-Centered Planning

typically includes some of the pertinent highlights of the person's history; a delineation of the person's preferences, interests, needs, strengths, current places, activities, and people who are important in the person's life (see Figure 4.1).

This personal profile provides the basis on which planning occurs, moving toward the articulation of a vision and goals for the future. For transition-age youth leaving high school, consider opportunities and goals related to transition domains including employment, recreation and leisure, home, community participation, and postsecondary training and education opportunities. Across these domains, it is important to identify skills and abilities that need to be developed in order to achieve the future goals. It is also important that the team prioritizes establishing a sense of belonging and developing personal relationships in these future contexts.

After the development of the personal profile and the articulation of hopes, dreams, and aspirations for the focus individual, it is important to identify both supports for and barriers to achievement of the preferred future. The team needs to brainstorm many possibilities and ideas, including identifying contacts who can support the dreams. Applying the "front door first" approach to the experience helps prioritize access to inclusive, typical pathways to postschool participation in age-appropriate roles, using natural supports, including resources available to all individuals before pursuing specialized services. The "front door first" approach promotes inclusion, authenticity, and self-advocacy in places of learning, employment settings, and local communities. Equally important, barriers to the individual's dreams need to be identified so that ideas for lessening or working around obstacles can be developed. Successful realization of dreams and goals is always a combination of taking advantage of supports and decreasing the effect of risk factors. Strategic planning includes an examination of all of the transition domains and essential elements.

CASE STUDY 4.1 (Collin)

Collin is an 18-year-old student with autism spectrum disorder participating in his public school's transition program. Collin's team engages in person-centered planning with the family and considers the environments where he will have opportunities to meet his desired outcomes after he graduates. Collin, his parents, and members of his team identify the specific environments available for working, playing, living, and learning. The team compiles information to include in Collin's Summary of Performance, which he plans to provide to the disability service office at the local college he hopes to attend. Collin's team continues to identify possible environments where he might choose to spend time. They also analyze these choices to figure out how to support him to experience a sense of belonging, develop personal relationships, and gain skills so that he can actively participate and contribute in these settings. Their goal is that ultimately he can achieve his personal vision. The team also decides to create a circle of support and utilize some supported decision-making strategies assigning trusted family members the role of assisting Collin with legal rights and daily decision making.

Research on Person-Centered Planning

Although there are numerous illustrations of how to use PCP, research is somewhat limited. Weir (2004) demonstrated that the PCP approach was critical to the realization of successful postsecondary education for transition-age individuals with significant disabilities. Effective practices, identified in Weir's study and applicable across various PCP approaches for both the creation and implementation of successful plans, include:

- Focus on the big picture.
- Proactively plan for change and celebrate success.
- Move purposefully, but do not rush through.
- Ensure outcome of the process is an actionable plan.

Using a PCP process supports the planning team's focus on the "big picture" and enables them to discuss issues important to the individual. Using the process pushes teams to attend to proactive long-term planning versus reactive short-term responding due to avoidance of planning. During initial planning, discussing things that may change in a person's life assists the planning team in identifying priorities and the best use of resources. Regularly revisit the plan to address changes and things to maintain. The identification of things to maintain leads to acknowledging and celebrating success for both the focus individual and the support team—always a positive thing to do to maintain needed energy.

Moving purposefully through the process to action ensures the planning team has adequate time for the discussions needed to keep the focus person's voice at the forefront and to create actionable high-expectation plans. Ensuring there is a plan that can be put into action is important. This is an area wherein PCP approaches vary in the specificity of action that results from the planning. Some approaches focus strongly on creating the personal profile and identifying future goals and opportunities and less on the actions needed to ensure that the plan is implemented with fidelity. Others are more specific and focus on what the individual will be doing and what support is required to engage in those activities and environments daily or weekly. Regardless of the PCP process used, it is important to articulate action steps. Equally important is that the team meet regularly, review activities, and make needed changes to support the realization of the vision.

Related specifically to transition from high school to adulthood, it is important for PCP to occur *before* a transition plan is written as part of the individualized education program (IEP). The rationale for this is that it is important to maintain the focus person at the center of planning and consider all domains of adult functioning to inform the transition plan. PCP includes individuals in the focus person's life beyond professionals, including family, friends, neighbors, co-workers, or others from the community (e.g., faith community, recreation center). Further, the outcome of the plan is to support the individual to not just be in the community, but to be a part of the community.

It is important for planning teams to know that this process will require a lot of hard work; they should not be deterred when challenges arise, but, rather, remain fully committed to the goal of supporting and empowering the focus person to have a fulfilling life in the community. PCP has been used for decades, but unfortunately is scarcely utilized. Successful implementation of PCP may require training that supports a high-expectations view of individuals with disabilities. Such training would need to support individuals with disabilities to be active participants for change in their own lives, rather than passive recipients of prescribed care (Buckles & Heimerl, 2016).

It is vital to understand that PCP is not just a one-time event anticipating an individual's exit from high school. Consider the many changes in jobs, living situations, and relationships that occur for most people across a lifetime. This same opportunity for change needs to be afforded those with disabilities. The focus individual must always be included in the planning process (whereas family, friends, professionals, and others who care about the person may change over time).

Barriers to Person-Centered Planning

The proposed outcome of PCP, a life in the community based upon individual preferences, interests, needs, strengths, and goals, includes several barriers (Joint Position Statement of AAIDD and AUCD, 2016). One barrier is simply access to community services; another is quality of these services. An example of a barrier to access is there may not be a home available that does not involve roommates chosen by others. In addition, there may not be opportunities for supported or competitive employment or access to technology that could increase an individual's ability to work, live, and recreate in the community.

In addition to simply accessing community services, there is wide variability in the quality of the choices and options of the community services available for individuals with disabilities. A tertiary challenge is the fact that funding for community living and working do not align with an individualized, person-centered model of support. Currently, more money is spent per person on institutionalized and segregated services than is spent on community living and supported employment (Joint Position Statement of AAIDD and AUCD, 2016).

Last, there are workforce challenges. Those paid to support individuals with disabilities in the community are sometimes underpaid and not provided training. This is not a good combination and often results in the direct-support workforce caretaking rather than holding high expectations and providing the support needed to assist individuals in becoming valued members of the competitive workforce, neighborhood, and community. When individuals with disabilities actively participate and contribute to the job market, they develop skills that enhance membership, respect, and contribution.

The field of education for individuals with disabilities has expanded in regard to expectation, opportunities, and possibilities for not just being in the community, but of the community. PCP is necessary for the realization of these expanded paradigms. The heart of PCP is to support youth to live their own lives, lives they choose, and lives that include fulfilling activities, relationships, and opportunities for contribution. To live a fulfilling and meaningful life is an outcome desired by all, and it should be no different for individuals with disabilities. PCP can make this a reality.

Summary of Performance

The Individuals With Disabilities Education Act (IDEA, 2006) requires schools to provide a Summary of Performance (SOP) to exiting students who have IEPs (IDEA Regulations, 2012, 34 CFR § 300.305[e][3]). Local education agencies create an SOP when special education eligibility is terminated due to a youth exceeding the state's age eligibility for a free and appropriate education or upon graduating with a high school diploma (National Secondary Transition Technical Assistance Center [NSTTAC], 2013). Federal regulations provide flexibility in determining content of an SOP but these should be based on a student's individual preferences, interests, needs, strengths, and postsecondary goals (Dukes, Shaw, & Madaus, 2007). The contents should include a summary of the student's academic achievement and functional performance and recommendations on how to meet postsecondary goals (Madaus, Bigaj, Chafouleas, & Simonsen, 2006).

To create the SOP, the IEP planning team gathers and organizes information from a number of sources and school personnel (e.g., special education teacher, general education teacher, school psychologist, related services personnel). To ensure the process is person-centered requires active involvement of the student and his or her family in the development of the document (Martin, Van Dycke, D'Ottavio, & Nickerson, 2007). Some states, school districts, and organizations have forms and templates with recommendations for the contents of an SOP. Table 4.1 provides suggested recommendations from the National Transition Documentation Summit (2005).

Table 4.1. Summary of Performance Contents

Element	Description
Background	Student's name, birth date, and graduation date
Disability	Student's primary and secondary disabilities and other relevant information from current IEP or Section 504 plan
Postsecondary goals	Transition goals that focus on the postsecondary environment(s) to which the student intends to transition upon completion of high school
Assessments[a]	Results of most recent formal and informal assessment to document the student's disability, strengths, and functional limitations to assist in postsecondary planning
Current performance	Summary of academic (reading, math, learning skills), cognitive (communication, attention), and functional levels of performance (social skills, mobility, self-determination)
Accommodations, modifications, and assistive technology	Strategies to assist the student in achieving progress
Recommendations	Essential and required supportive services to enhance access in a postsecondary environment and assist the individual in meeting postsecondary goals; may include higher education, training, employment, independent living, and community participation

Note. IEP = individualized education program.
[a]Although many institutions of higher education and state agencies require current information about a student's disability, IDEA does not require a reevaluation at the time a student graduates from high school or ages out of public education.

The SOP process serves multiple purposes (Project Forum, 2008) including the opportunity to:

- Provide postsecondary settings with measures of a student's current performance and recommended accommodations for use in those settings.
- Highlight student's strengths.
- Empower student to self-advocate.
- Help student achieve his or her postsecondary goals and enhance postsecondary outcomes.
- Facilitate development of a plan for student's employment under vocational rehabilitation services.

Per IDEA, the SOP must be prepared during the final year of a student's secondary education to provide information to those who may assist the student in the future (NSTTAC, 2013). If a student transitions to higher education, a comprehensive SOP provides information on current level of functioning and how to best provide supports, accommodations, and access under Section 504 of the Rehabilitation Act and the Americans with Disabilities Act. A well-constructed SOP (Shaw, Keenan, Madaus, & Banerjee. 2010) will provide:

- Strong evidence of the current functional impact of a disability on a student.
- Academic accommodations that have been utilized.
- Extent to which such accommodations have been effective.

Likewise, this information may serve useful as a student applies for employment services from state agencies such as vocational rehabilitation. The SOP should be viewed as a blueprint to help pave the way for a youth's seamless transition from secondary education to postsecondary education, training, and employment (Kochhar-Bryant, 2007).

Guardianship

Guardianship is something that families need to consider as a child reaches the age of majority, which is the legal age determined by state law where youth are legally responsible for their choices and actions (Millar, 2013). It is important that the individual with the disability, family members, and educators understand that parents do not automatically remain guardians of an adult son or daughter because of a disability, and only a court order can appoint a guardian for someone upon the age of majority (Millar, 2014). In a school setting, guardianship is a topic typically discussed during transition-related IEP meetings. At the age of majority, all rights transfer from the parents to the student unless the student is determined by state law to be incompetent or considered to lack the capacity to provide informed consent (34 C.F.R. § 300.517; Millar, 2014).

Informed consent is defined as an individual's "ability to make knowledgeable choices about programs, procedures, or activities that are potentially invasive or have significant impact on that person's life" (Lindsey, Wehmeyer, Guy, & Martin, 2001, p.6). Informed consent implies that the individual understands how to (a) gather adequate information about an issue, (b) predict the consequences of an action, (c) use information to make decisions, (d) give permission, and (e) participate voluntarily (Lindsey et al., 2001).

Guardianship is a process where a petition is made to a court to assign an individual to make decisions on behalf of someone who is perceived as unable to do so (Jameson et al., 2015; Quality Trust for Individuals with Disabilities, 2014).

The person determined to be "incompetent" or "incapacitated" (Dore, 2008), that is, incapable of making daily living decisions, is referred to as a "ward" and the individual who is given legal permission to make decisions for the ward is the court-appointed guardian (Millar, 2014). A developmental disability by itself is typically not enough to demonstrate that the individual lacks the capacity to make sound decisions, perform certain functions, and control his or her own life (Millar, 2014). Because guardianship involves a loss of freedom, state laws may require that guardianship be imposed only when less restrictive alternatives have been tried and found ineffective.

Ultimately, guardianship attempts to ensure that vulnerable persons are protected and quality of life is improved (Flower, 1994; Welber, 2005). Guardians can decide living arrangements, handle daily finances, decide medical treatments, and make other life decisions with the aim of protecting the rights of the individual with a disability (Froemming & Abramson, 2000). In some cases, parents or caretakers view guardianship as necessary due to concerns for the individual with the disability (e.g., unable to protect oneself, limited cognitive ability; Dinnerstein, Herr, & O'Sullivan, 1999). In other cases, parents or caretakers may not seek guardianship and willingly surrender authority to the courts or allow the individual to make all of his or her own decisions (Hoyle, 2005). Nevertheless, research is limited when it comes to finding and supporting the benefits of guardianship for individuals with disabilities (Jameson et al., 2015). The sections that follow describe different approaches and effective guardianship practices related to protecting individuals with disabilities and their rights.

Plenary and Partial Guardianship

With guardianship, an individual's right to make decisions or perform functions is affected (Coleman & Nerney, 2005). For example, guardianship may remove an individual's entitlement to vote (Self-Advocates Becoming Empowered, 2017). Courts can assign plenary, partial, or limited guardianship of individuals with disabilities (Jameson et al., 2015). Plenary or full guardianship typically lasts throughout the individual's life and guardians may make all decisions for the individual with the disability (Millar, 2013). Partial or limited guardianship may be for a limited time (Millar & Renzaglia, 2002) and may allow persons to maintain and make independent choices (Millar, 2013).

Circles of Support

Coleman and Nerney (2005) stressed that one should focus on "assisted competence." Circles of support could be used as an alternative to guardianship to provide assisted competence to an individual with a disability. Circles of support can help an individual with a disability make decisions, voice preferences, and participate in decision making (Coleman & Nerney, 2005). The circles are networks consisting of the person with a disability and others who care about the individual's well-being (Stansberry Brusnahan, 2014). The circles should consist of individuals beyond the immediate family and friends, such as local community members. Individuals involved in the support circles work together to ensure quality of life by meeting with the person to (a) discuss challenges in terms of daily life, (b) ensure access and navigation to supports (e.g., eligibility-specific goods and services, community supports, relationship-based supports, technology), (c) plan opportunities to reach goals, and (d) carry out activities within the community (Barrett & Randall, 2004; Frederickson, Warren, & Turner, 2005). The circles should focus on assisting the individual in areas that are needed, such as advocacy, self-determination, healthy living, citizenship, community living, safety, spirituality, social, and employment.

Supported Decision Making

Supported decision making is an alternative to guardianship where individuals with disabilities have supporters who *help* them make their *own* choices. Supported decision making awards trusted friends or family members the role of assisting an adult with legal rights and daily decision making (Jameson et al., 2015). However, the individual with the disability maintains control of the final decision (Jameson et al., 2015; Quality Trust for Individuals with Disabilities, 2014). Supported decisions are considered legally binding, yet relationships can be terminated at any time by the person with a disability (Salzman, 2010).

Power of Attorney

Power of attorney allocates an individual to make minor and major life decisions for a person. Approval is given only when an individual completely understands what is being asked, and a designated person with power of attorney can make decisions with recommendations from the individual (Millar, 2007). Power of attorney permits families to assist with decision making. It can be revoked at any time and does not require guardianship to be established (Agoratus, 2014).

Appointed Representative Payee

There are alternatives to guardianship when financial assets are involved. If an individual receives benefits of any type and has difficulty handling funds, a representative payee can be appointed to handle personal finances (UMKC

Institute for Human Development, 2014). The appointee disburses the money or funds and keeps a record of all disbursements on behalf of the individual (Social Security Administration, 2017).

Special Needs Trust

A special needs trust is advantageous when an individual receives large sums of money that may impact benefits from Supplemental Security Income or Medicaid (Harris, 2005). A trust is an alternative to guardianship wherein a trustee helps manage assets such as basic necessities, food, clothing, and shelter (UMKC Institute for Human Development, 2010). The trustee can assist or hire a third party to ensure a person's overall well-being and quality of life is maintained (Welber, 2005).

Money Managing Supports

Bank accounts can be set up to maintain supervision over an individual's finances and spending money (UMKC Institute for Human Development, 2010; Millar, 2007). Examples of money managing supports include direct deposit and automatic bill pay. Other supports might include cosigners or joint accounts (Millar, 2007).

Families and professionals need information about guardianship (Hoyle, 2005). Often, guardianship is recommended as the only approach and families can be pressured into guardianship, particularly when presented with scary scenarios (Hoyle, 2005). The decision must be weighed carefully, since it greatly influences the future of the young adult with a disability. As such, it is essential that parents understand exactly what guardianship entails. All individuals with disabilities must be provided their rights before reaching the age of majority (IDEA, 2004). However, it is critical to determine and subsequently raise any concerns before reaching adulthood. The Guardianship Alternative Assessment Template (Millar, 2014) helps explore an individual's vision, ideals, daily living skills, cognitive abilities, safety concerns, alternatives, and means to improve competence. Collaborative processes between professionals and families help educate parents and increase an individual's quality of life (Hoyle, 2005). Involving family and friends in matters can help ensure life decisions meet the individual's life goals and expectations. Circles of support, supported decision making, and other alternatives to guardianship help the individual with a disability maintain autonomy.

Summary

This chapter highlighted the topics of PCP, SOP, and guardianship as they relate to transition-age students with disabilities. Education teams can utilize PCP to support students with disabilities in identifying what they would define as a high quality of life and developing goals to bring that purpose and meaning to life. Schools are required to create an SOP for a student with an IEP prior to exiting high school (NSTTAC, 2013). The summary of current performance and recommendations can assist the student with a disability in meeting higher education or employment postsecondary goals. When a student is about to reach the state's age of majority, educators should share information on guardianship with the family. When appropriate, a family can request that a court assign a guardian to make decisions on behalf of the child or seek alternatives to guardianship to support the youth being a self-advocate with the right to communicate choice and make decisions (Harris, 2005). Ultimately, the processes and practices discussed in this chapter can be used to help protect an individual with a disability's rights and promote a person-centered smooth transition from school into adulthood.

References

Agoratus, L. (2014). Financial planning: Alternatives to guardianship. *EP Magazine, 44*(11), 30–31.

Barrett, W., & Randall, L. (2004). Investigating the circle of friends approach: Adaptations and implications for practice. *Educational Psychology in Practice, 20*, 353–367. doi:10.1080/0266736042000314286

Bolding, N., Wehmeyer, M. L., & Lawrence, M. (2010). *It's my future! Planning for what I want in my life—A self-directed planning process.* Retrieved from http://ngsd.org/sites/default/files/its_my_future.pdf

Buckles, J., & Heimerl, C. (2016). Building support that creates community: Person-centered supports in New Mexico. *IMPACT Newsletter, 29*, 29–30.

Coleman, D., & Nerney, T. (2005). Guardianship and the disability rights movement. *TASH Connections, 31*, 16–19.

Dinnerstein, R. D., Herr, S. S., & O'Sullivan, J. L. (1999). *A guide to consent.* Washington, DC: American Association of Mental Retardation.

Dore, M. K. (2008). Ten reasons people get railroaded into guardianship. *American Journal of Family Law, 21*, 148–152.

Dukes, L., Shaw, S., & Madaus, J. (2007). How to compete a summary of performance for students exiting to postsecondary education. *Assessment for Effective Intervention, 32*, 143–159. doi:10.1177/15345084070320030301

Flower, D. (1994). Guardianship and self-determination. *IMPACT Newsletter, 6*, 15–16.

Frederickson, N., Warren, L., & Turner, J. (2005). "Circle of friends"—An exploration of impact over time. *Educational Psychology in Practice, 21*, 197–217. doi:10.1080/02667360500205883

Froemming, R., & Abramson, B. (2000). *Guardianship of adults: A decision making guide for family members, friends and advocates*. Madison: Wisconsin Department of Health and Family Services, Division of Supportive Living. Retrieved from https://www.co.brown.wi.us/i_brown/d/aging_disability_resource_center/guardianship_booklet_from_wi_website.pdf

Griffin, M. M., McMillan, E. D., & Hodapp, R. M. (2010). Family perspectives on postsecondary education for students with intellectual disabilities. *Education and Training in Autism and Developmental Disabilities, 45*, 339–346.

Harris, K. (2005). Guardianship is not self-determination. *TASH Connections, 31*, 22–23.

Hoyle, D. (2005). Eliminating the pervasiveness of guardianship. *TASH Connections, 31*, 14–15.

IDEA regulations, 34 C.F.R. § 300 (2012).

Individuals With Disabilities Education Act, 20 U.S.C. §§ 1400 *et seq*. (2006 & Supp. V. 2011)

Jameson, J. M., Riesen, T., Polychronis, S., Trader, B., Martinis, J., Mizner, S., & Hoyle, D. (2015). Guardianship and the potential of supported decision making with individuals with disabilities. *Research and Practice for Persons with Severe Disabilities, 40*, 1–16. doi:10.1177/1540796915586189

Joint Position Statement of AAIDD and AUCD. (2016, June). *Community living and participation for people with intellectual and development disabilities*. Retrieved from http://aaidd.org/news-policy/policy/position-statements/community-living-and-participation#.WmY-EiOZMW8

Kochhar-Bryant, C. (2007). The summary of performance as transition passport to employment and independent living. *Assessment for Effective Intervention, 32*, 160–170. doi:10.1177/15345084070320030401

Lindsey, P., Wehmeyer, M. L., Guy, B., & Martin, J. (2001). Age of majority and mental retardation: A position statement of the division on mental retardation and developmental disabilities. *Education and Training in Mental Retardation and Developmental Disabilities 36*, 3–15.

Madaus, J., Bigaj, S., Chafouleas, S., & Simonsen, B. (2006). What key information can be included in a comprehensive summary of performance? *Career Development for Exceptional Individuals, 29*, 90–99. doi:10.1177/08857288 060290020701

Martin, J., Van Dycke, J., D'Ottavio, M., & Nickerson, K. (2007). The student-directed summary of performance: Increasing student and family involvement in the transition planning process. *Career Development for Exceptional Individuals, 30*, 13–26. doi:10.1177/08857288070300010101

Millar, D. S. (2007). "I never put it together": The disconnect between self-determination and guardianship—implications for practice. *Education and Training in Development Disabilities, 42*, 119–129.

Millar, D. S. (2013). Guardianship alternatives: Their use affirms self-determination of individuals with intellectual disabilities. *Education and Training in Autism and Developmental Disabilities, 48*, 291–305.

Millar, D. S. (2014). Addition to transition assessment resources: A template for determining the use of guardianship alternatives for students who have intellectual disability. *Education and Training in Autism and Developmental Disabilities, 49*, 171–188.

Millar, D. S., & Renzaglia, A. (2002). Factors affecting guardianship practices for young adults with disabilities. *Exceptional Children, 68*, 465–484. doi:10.1177/001440290206800404

National Secondary Transition Technical Assistance Center. (2013). *Summary of performance resources.* Retrieved from http://www.nsttac.org/content/summary-performance-resources

National Transition Documentation Summit. (2005). *Summary of performance model template.* Retrieved from http://www.wrightslaw.com/info/trans.sop.template.pdf

New Jersey Coalition for Inclusive Education. (2013). *Plotting your course: A guide to using the MAPS process for planning inclusive opportunities and facilitating transitions.* Retrieved from http://njcie.org/portfolio-item/plotting-course-guide-using-maps-process/

Pearpoint, J., O'Brien, J., & Forest, M. (1993). *Planning possible positive futures (PATH): Planning alternative tomorrows with hope for schools, organizations, businesses, and families.* Toronto, Canada: Inclusion Press.

Project Forum. (2008). *Summary of performance.* Retrieved from http://nasdse.org/DesktopModules/DNNspot-Store/ProductFiles/112_c73c7942-deb9-446e-b27e-7570eac1f33a.pdf

Quality Trust for Individuals with Disabilities. (2014). *Supported decision-making: An agenda for action.* Retrieved from http://bbi.syr.edu/news_events/news/2014/02/Supported%20Decision%20Making-2014.pdf

Salzman, L. (2010). Rethinking guardianship (again): Substituted decision making as a violation of the integration mandate of Title II of the Americans With Disabilities Act. University of *Colorado Law Review, 81,* 157–244.

Self-Advocates Becoming Empowered. (2017). *Voting and guardianship.* Retrieved from http://www.sabeusa.org/voting-and-guardianship/

Shaw, S. F., Keenan, W. R., Madaus, J. W., & Banerjee, M. (2010). Disability documentation, the Americans With Disabilities Act Amendments Act, and the summary of performance: How are they linked? *Association of Higher Education and Disability (AHEAD) Journal of Postsecondary Education and Disability, 22,* 142– 150. Retrieved from http://files.eric.ed.gov/fulltext/EJ906687.pdf

Social Security Administration. (2017). *When people need help managing their money.* Retrieved from https://www.ssa.gov/payee/

Stansberry Brusnahan, L. L. (2014). Creating circles of natural social supports: Impact on adult with autism spectrum disorder's quality of life. *Division on Autism and Developmental Disabilities Online Journal, 1,* 166–182.

Thompson, J. R., Bryant, B. R., Schalock, R. L., Shogren, K. A., Tassé, M. J., Wehmeyer, M. L., ... Rotholz, D. A. (2015). *Supports Intensity Scale—Adult Version.* Washington, DC: American Association on Intellectual and Developmental Disabilities.

Thompson, J. R., Doepke, K., Homes, A., Pratt, C., Smith Myles, B., Shogren, K. A., & Wehmeyer, M. (2017). *Person-centered planning with the SIS-A: A guide for planning teams.* Washington, DC: American Association on Intellectual and Developmental Disabilities.

Timmons, J., Freeman, R., Olson, M., Benway, C., & Gulaid, A. (2016). A model for building a statewide infrastructure for person-centered practices and positive supports: Minnesota's approach. *IMPACT Newsletter, 29*(2), 36–39.

UMKC Institute for Human Development, Disability and Health Information Center. (2010). *Missouri guardianship: Understanding your options & alternatives.* Retrieved from https://health.mo.gov/CSHCN/docs/GuardianshipInfoPack.pdf

Wehmeyer, M., Lawrence, M., Kelchner, K., Palmer, S., Garner, N., & Soukup, J. (2004). *Whose future is it anyway? A student-directed transition planning process* (2nd ed.). Lawrence, KS: Beach Center on Disability.

Weir, C. (2004). Person-centered and collaborative supports for college success. *Education and Training in Developmental Disabilities, 39*, 67–73.

Welber, J. S. (2005). The trust as an alternative to guardianship. *TASH Connections, 31*, 29–31.

CHAPTER 5
Preparing Students for Inclusive Postschool Settings
Leslie K. O. Okoji, Sean Nagamatsu, Robert A. Stodden, and Eric Folk

Objectives:
- Highlight the importance and significance of inclusive settings.
- Present the framework for supporting youth with disabilities in transitioning to inclusive postschool settings.
- Provide best practices focused on inclusive skill development and meaningful strategies that lead to a successful transition to inclusive postschool settings.

This chapter focuses on preparing students for transition into inclusive postschool settings, and the importance and significance of inclusive settings in and beyond high schools for youth with developmental disabilities, including those with autism spectrum disorder and intellectual disability. Chapter 5 includes a discussion of a best-practice framework to support transition to inclusive postschool options, and provides strategies that lead to inclusive skill development and successful transition to postschool settings. Secondary schools are the ideal setting to provide support and services that focus on the acquisition and use of skills and knowledge that build on independence and sustainability. Incorporating a person-centered approach to transition planning for life after high school (see Chapters 3 and 4) creates an opportunity for educators to foster high expectations and seek out ways to create more meaningful, inclusive experiences for students.

Key Terminology	
21st-century skills	Skills that promote a self-determined and meaningful life. These skills consist of essential content knowledge (core academic subjects), as well as (a) learning and innovation skills; (b) information and technology skills; and (c) career and life skills. (Partnership for 21st Century Learning, 2015).

Key Terminology (cont'd)	
Inclusion	An education setting in which "all students are full and accepted members of their school community" (Inclusive Schools Network, 2017); students with disabilities are educated alongside and have opportunities to interact with their typically developing peers.
Independent living skills	The foundational skills needed for an individual to be able to live independently (e.g., household, money management, personal health, hygiene, meal management, mobility).

Supporting youth with disabilities' inclusion in the high school setting is twofold: It starts with promoting inclusive academic and social settings, and it continues with providing person-centered transition opportunities alongside peers. Research has shown that inclusion in general education core curriculum, paid employment work experience, self-care and independent living skills, and student support predict improved postschool outcomes in employment, education, and independent living for students with developmental and intellectual disabilities (Kurth, Lyon, & Shogren, 2015; Mazzotti et al., 2016; Odom, Buysse, & Soukakou, 2011; Test et al., 2009). Research has also shown that students with autism spectrum disorder and those with severe disabilities benefit in academic and "soft" skills development in inclusive settings (Kurth & Mastergeorge, 2012). Soft skills, such as communication, socialization, and self-determination, are important for postschool options, including employment and postsecondary success (Kurth & Mastergeorge, 2010; Kurth et al., 2015).

Inclusive settings provide the real-life context for students to draw upon meaningful experiences and skills to succeed in postschool goals. Without these skills and experiences, postschool options for young adults with disabilities are limited—due to settings that provide minimal preparation for integrated employment (Butler, Sheppard-Jones, Whaley, Harrison, & Osness, 2016) and few opportunities to participate in inclusive postsecondary education (Grigal & Hart, 2013; Grigal, Hart, & Weir, 2012; Plotner & Marshall, 2015; Uditsky & Hughson, 2012). For individuals with disabilities, accessing opportunities and supports and participating in inclusive settings may be a critical pathway to meaningful employment, community involvement, and social acceptance (Stodden, Brown, Galloway, Mrazek, & Noy, 2005).

In federal education law and regulations regarding youth with disabilities, the word *inclusion* has been associated with the principle of "least restrictive environment," and indicates the preference for students with disabilities to be educated with necessary aids and supports in general education settings alongside their typical peers. Recent federal policy offered guidance on providing meaningful, inclusive settings and experiences in early childhood programs, yet stopped short of discussing inclusion as being all encompassing (U.S. Department of Health and Human Services and U.S. Department of Education, 2015). *Inclusive education* is a setting in which all students have a sense of belonging because they are "full and accepted" members of their school community (Inclusive Schools Network, 2017), and students participate in the same education settings as their same-age peers. This position is a mindset shift that frames the framework and strategies presented in this chapter.

As secondary students transition to postschool environments, they will naturally encounter inclusive settings such as postsecondary education, employment, and other social settings. For this reason, it is imperative that high school youth with disabilities are supported by an inclusive curriculum, standards-based core academic subject skills and nonacademic skills (e.g., 21st-century skills), and early transition planning with collaborative teams to prepare for postschool options.

Inclusive Curriculum

A shift in thinking is fundamental to address the disparity of education placements for youth with disabilities. Individualized education program (IEP) teams should not only consider but advocate for options other than segregated, self-contained classrooms. Studies have shown that high-quality instruction employing evidence-based strategies (e.g., prompts, visuals, assistive technology, universal design, coaching) in inclusive classrooms are effective ways to support students with disabilities in the general education setting (Ehren & Little, 2014; Kurth et al., 2015). In addition, creative and nontraditional teaching arrangements and collaboration such as co-teaching have been shown to support all students in inclusive settings (Ehren & Little, 2014; Kurth et al., 2015). Finally, inclusive classrooms provide the real-life context for age-appropriate social engagement, where genuine and reciprocal friendships across abilities can form (Kurth et al., 2015).

Academic and Nonacademic Skills

Educators should utilize a diverse, contextualized curriculum that is integrated with core academic classes to address functional living skills (Stodden, Abhari, & Kong, 2015). Many students with disabilities need continued support and integrated instruction in functional, daily living skills to increase independence after high school (Ayres, Alisa, Douglas, & Sievers, 2011; Shogren, Palmer, Wehmeyer, Williams-Diehm, & Little, 2011). Providing integrated instruction in functional curriculum areas with core academic skills has been effective in helping students develop independent skills and to be college and career ready (Ayres et al., 2011). This approach to addressing functional skill development as identified in transition plans can contribute to improved graduation rates and successful transition to postschool settings (Benz, Lindstrom, & Yovanoff, 2000).

Recently, leaders in education, business, and policy worked together to spearhead a movement emphasizing the need for 21st-century life skills, considered necessary for all students to prosper as adults. These skills encompass key subjects and 21st-century themes, including learning and innovation skills; information, media, and technology skills; and life and career skills (Partnership for 21st Century Learning, 2015). Current curriculum should include a contextualized focus of diverse 21st-century life skills that prepare students at all abilities to be successful in the community and school (Agran, Wehmeyer, Cavin, & Palmer, 2010; Morningstar, Lombardi, Fowler, & Test, 2015; Stodden et al., 2015) and to accomplish their long-term aspirations and goals (U.S. Department of Education, 2015).

Collaborative Transition Planning

Along with providing appropriate inclusive curriculum to address academic and nonacademic skills, secondary schools play an important role in connecting students and their families to appropriate adult agencies and services. Early interagency collaborative teaming is critical in successful transition planning to postschool options (Folk, Yamamoto, & Stodden, 2012; Stodden et al., 2015; Yamamoto, Stodden, & Folk, 2014) and is being used more frequently as a framework to support students with disabilities in their personal and educational goals (Noonan, Erickson, McCall, Frey, & Zheng, 2014). Collaborative teaming among agencies can support students in meaningful person-centered plans, and focus on the development of self-determination and independence (Foley, Dyke, Girdler, Bourke, & Leonard, 2012; Folk et al., 2012; Yamamoto et al., 2014).

The role of secondary educators in coordinating interagency teams and incorporating person-centered plans is vital to the transition to inclusive postschool options (Stodden et al., 2015; Yamamoto et al., 2014). Educators can assist students in identifying their own needs and help students learn how to advocate for appropriate services based on self-determined goals. Equally important is helping students and families understand the types of services available after leaving high school. The amount and type of postschool services and accommodations can greatly differ from the wrap-around services provided through the Individuals With Disabilities Education Act (IDEA, 2006). With a collaborative teaming approach to transition, secondary schools can provide the bridge to assist students and families in navigating adult agencies and postsecondary education systems.

These valuable connections, made during high school, link the student with the necessary resources, services, and supports to employment, education, and other postschool options related to the student's self-determined goals. Community or other state agencies can offer opportunities for students to learn both academic and nonacademic skills in inclusive and real-life settings and should be included as valued members of the transition team.

CASE STUDY 5.1 (Kawika)

Kawika is an 18-year-old high school senior with an intellectual disability who participates on his school's football team and has many friends on campus. As a junior, he participated in full inclusion settings for all of his classes except for math and English. His self-advocacy for inclusion in these subject areas proved a valuable learning experience that helped Kawika prepare for postsecondary education.

With the encouragement of his special education teacher, Kawika requested to be in full inclusion classes for the entirety of his senior-year schedule, which led to his enrollment in high-quality curriculum in math and English designed to meet all learners' needs. This included maintaining high standards and using rubrics to clearly define expectations for all students. At first, Kawika struggled to keep up with the demands of the classes, so strategies such as chunking and preteaching helped teachers support him in understanding and completing his assignments.

In both classes, students utilized laptops extensively in their learning. The teachers organized students into pairs, which helped Kawika make up for his little prior knowledge and use of technical devices. Paired students were taught ways to provide constructive feedback for each other, to problem solve, and to ask for further assistance. This pairing-and-sharing strategy was used for all students and not singled out for Kawika. The teachers saw improvement in all students' understanding of the content and increased communication and interaction skills.

During Kawika's collaborative team meeting, his general education teachers shared this approach to curriculum and instruction. Kawika's Vocational Rehabilitation counselor was able to provide a personal laptop to support his continued growth in 21st-century skills, as well as in math, English, and other subjects. In addition, his counselor set up a series of appointments with Kawika to assist him in preparation for postsecondary education based on his success in inclusion settings.

A Best-Practice Framework

Recent federal initiatives and the development of inclusive curricula in secondary schools have advanced opportunities for more students to participate in inclusive settings, including postsecondary education (Papay & Bambara, 2011). Improved support for secondary educators; comprehensive transition planning; and interagency partnerships among secondary schools, employers, parents, students, and postsecondary institutions have helped to ignite new research and model demonstrations to inform policy and systems change (Folk et al., 2012; Stodden & Dowrick, 2000).

The framework that was presented in Chapter 1 is designed to support and expand inclusive postschool opportunities that promote acquisition of self-determination, independent living, employment, and soft skills for youth with developmental disabilities, including autism spectrum disorder and intellectual disability (Folk et al., 2012). The preparation for postschool options begins in secondary school settings. The framework's components foster inclusive practices in postschool environments, and incorporate the concept of "front door first" and the use of adaptive coaching to support inclusion.

"Front Door First" Approach to Inclusion

The "front door first" approach prioritizes student access to inclusive and typical pathways to postschool participation using natural supports. The focus is on utilizing resources available to all students prior to pursuing specialized services. This approach promotes inclusion, authenticity, and self-advocacy in students and facilitates awareness about the presence and needs of diverse learners on postsecondary campuses, at places of employment, and in places in the community.

Adaptive Coaching

Adaptive coaches support participants to pursue inclusive opportunities beyond high school, provide one-to-one strategy coaching, and give valuable feedback to students. Adaptive coaching is personal interaction between a support person and the student. The focus is on assisting students to successfully pursue and participate in inclusive academic, social, and employment opportunities at school or in the community. The adaptive coach focuses on a variety of skills and content related to personal goals, strengths, and needs. Coaches work to empower students to build their capacity to grow independently and to transition successfully to postschool opportunities.

As illustrated in Table 5.1, coaches play a variety of roles in their interactions with students based on the individual needs of the students in a secondary school setting. These roles may include academic, social skills, system navigation, employment coaching, organization and time management assistance, and supporting the development of executive functioning and self-management skills. At the secondary school level, the coaching role can be assumed by natural supports such as classroom teachers, aides, or trained peers. These natural supports in inclusive environments also provide a wealth of resources to students with and without disabilities, do not require additional funding sources, and can be easily incorporated into an educator's compilation of strategies (Folk et al., 2012).

Table 5.1. Adaptive Coaching Strategies

Area of support	Strategies	Examples
Academics	Differentiate classroom instruction	Prompts and sentence starters, chunking, pre-teaching main concepts, guided notes
	Assist students in understanding course organization	Syllabi, deadlines, grade weights, submission procedures, classroom expectations
	Help students develop academic skills	Test-taking strategies, memory strategies, note taking, active participation strategies
Interactions and communication	Assess and broaden student awareness of natural supports and services in the environment	Academic advisors, teachers, school counseling, peer tutors or coaches, athletic coaches, church members, family members, community agencies, financial literacy workshops, college and career fairs, internship opportunities, career centers
	Promote self-determination through increased independence and assertiveness skills	Value student voice, introduce a variety of means for communicating needs and wants
	Guide students in managing supports and opportunities in an organized schedule	Coordinating with instructors for assistance, planning transportation, using a planner

Table 5.1. Adaptive Coaching Strategies (cont'd)		
Area of support	**Strategies**	**Examples**
Interactions and communication (cont'd)	Assist students in developing effective communication skills	Practicing scripts before communicating with natural supports, developing email and phone communication
	Teach students to research resources to help with physical and systems navigation	College campus maps, building floorplans, bus maps, online neighborhood maps, help desks, information booths
	Discuss various sets of expectations	Postsecondary education, workplace, community settings
	Introduce and apply appropriate interaction and communication skills across different postschool settings	Accepting and giving feedback to others, seeking assistance, solving problems, making decisions, resolving conflicts, working independently and in groups
	Teach and reinforce skills for successful school and work habits	Phone, text, email communication; planner and calendar use; mobile device reminders and alarms
Technology	Teach students effective digital practices	Accessing and assessing reliability of information, utilizing safe and legal online social interactions, keeping data secure
	Teach students how to use assistive technology and access resources	Text-to-speech/speech-to-text, online academic activities and resources
	Maintain a database of mobile applications (apps) that help develop academic, independence, and employment skills	Time management, calendars, prioritization, motivation, note taking, to-do lists, reminders, study tools, dictionaries, thesaurus

Summary

Providing natural supports and high expectations in an inclusive framework brings together the important components for skill development and successful transition to postschool settings for individuals with disabilities. Individual strategies within a framework of the "front door first" approach and adaptive coaching represent the explicit actions secondary educators can apply to prepare students for inclusive postschool settings. Continued advocacy for inclusion, high-quality curricula that focuses on academic and nonacademic 21st-century skill development, and person-centered approaches to transition planning provides the foundation for positive outcomes, broadens postschool options available, and ultimately changes the trajectory of a person's journey.

References

Agran, M., Wehmeyer, M., Cavin, M., & Palmer, S. (2010). Promoting active engagement in the general education classroom and access to the general education curriculum for students with cognitive disabilities. *Education and Training in Autism and Developmental Disabilities, 45*, 163–174.

Ayres, K. M., Alisa, L. K., Douglas, K. H., & Sievers, C. (2011). I can identify Saturn but I can't brush my teeth: What happens when the curricular focus for students with severe disabilities shifts. *Education and Training in Autism and Developmental Disabilities, 46*, 11–21.

Benz, M. R., Lindstrom, L., & Yovanoff, P. (2000). Improving graduation and employment outcomes of students with disabilities: Predictive factors and student perspectives. *Exceptional Children, 66*, 509–529. doi:10.1177/001440290006600405

Butler, L. N., Sheppard-Jones, K., Whaley, B., Harrison, B., & Osness, M. (2016). Does participation in higher education make a difference in life outcomes for students with intellectual disability? *Journal of Vocational Rehabilitation, 44*, 295–298. doi:10.3233/JVR-160804

Ehren, B., & Little, M. E. (2014). High school inclusion for the 21st century. In J. McLeskey, N. L. Waldron, F. Spooner, & B. Algozzine (Eds.), *Handbook of effective inclusive schools: Research and practice* (pp. 322–336). New York, NY: Routledge.

Foley, K. R., Dyke, P., Girdler, S., Bourke, J., & Leonard, H. (2012). Young adults with intellectual disability transitioning from school to postschool: A literature review framed within the ICF. *Disability and Rehabilitation, 34*, 1747–1764. doi:10.3109/09638288.2012.660603

Folk, E. R., Yamamoto, K. K., & Stodden, R. A. (2012). Implementing inclusion and collaborative teaming in a model program of postsecondary education for young adults with intellectual disabilities. *Journal of Policy & Practice in Intellectual Disabilities, 9*, 257–269. doi:10.1111/jppi.12007

Grigal, M., & Hart, D. (2013) Transition and postsecondary education programs for students with intellectual disability: A pathway to employment. *Think College Fast Facts, Issue No. 4.* Boston: University of Massachusetts, Institute for Community Inclusion.

Grigal, M., Hart, D., & Weir, C. (2012). A survey of postsecondary education programs for students with intellectual disabilities in the United States. *Journal of Policy & Practice in Intellectual Disabilities, 9*, 223–233. doi:10.1111/jppi.12012

Inclusive Schools Network. (2017). *Inclusion basics*. Retrieved from http://inclusiveschools.org/category/resources/inclusion-basics/

Individuals With Disabilities Education Act, 20 U.S.C. §§ 1400 *et seq*. (2006 & Supp. V. 2011)

Kurth, J., & Mastergeorge, A. M. (2010). Individual education plan goals and services for adolescents with autism: Impact of age and educational setting. *The Journal of Special Education, 44*, 146–160. doi:10.1177/0022466908329825

Kurth, J., & Mastergeorge, A. M. (2012). Impact of setting and instructional context for adolescents with autism. *The Journal of Special Education, 46*, 36–48. doi:10.1177/0022466910366480

Kurth, J. A., Lyon, K. J., & Shogren, K. A. (2015). Supporting students with severe disabilities in inclusive schools. *Research & Practice for Persons with Severe Disabilities, 40*, 261–274. doi:10.1177/1540796915594160

Mazzotti, V. L., Rowe, D. A., Sinclair, J., Poppen, M., Woods, W. E., & Shearer, M. L. (2016). Predictors of postschool success: A systematic review of NLTS2 secondary analyses. *Career Development and Transition for Exceptional Individuals, 39*, 196–215. doi:10.1177/2165143415588047

Morningstar, M. E., Lombardi, A., Fowler, C. H., & Test, D. W. (2015). A college and career readiness framework for secondary students with disabilities. *Career Development and Transition for Exceptional Individuals, 40*, 1-13. doi:10.1177/2165143415589926

Noonan, P., Erickson, A. G., McCall, Z., Frey, B. B., & Zheng, C. (2014). Evaluating change in interagency collaboration of a state-level interagency education team: A social network approach within a utilization-focused framework. *Educational Assessment, Evaluation and Accountability, 26*, 301–316. doi:10.1007/s11092-014-9193-2

Odom, S. L., Buysse, V., & Soukakou, E. (2011). Inclusion for young children with disabilities: A quarter century of research perspectives. *Journal of Early Intervention, 33*, 344–356. doi:10.1177/1053815111430094

Papay, C. K., & Bambara, L. M. (2011). Postsecondary education for transition-age students with intellectual and other developmental disabilities: A national survey. *Education and Training in Autism and Developmental Disabilities, 46*, 78–93.

Partnership for 21st Century Learning. (2015, May). *P21 framework definitions*. Retrieved from http://www.p21.org/storage/documents/docs/P21_Framework_Definitions_New_Logo_2015.pdf

Plotner, A. J., & Marshall, K. J. (2015). Postsecondary education programs for students with an intellectual disability: Facilitators and barriers to implementation. *Intellectual & Developmental Disabilities, 53*, 58–69. doi:10.1352/1934-9556-53.1.58

Shogren, K. A., Palmer, S. B., Wehmeyer, M. L., Williams-Diehm, K., & Little, T. (2011). Effect of intervention with the *Self-Determined Learning Model of Instruction* on access and goal attainment. *Remedial and Special Education, 33*, 320–330. doi:10.1177/0741932511410072

Stodden, R. A., Abhari, K., & Kong, E. (2015). Secondary school preparation and transition of youth with disabilities. In B. G. Cook, M. Tankersley, & T. J. Landrum (Eds.), *Transition of youth and young adults* (pp. 7–30). Bingley, England: Emerald.

Stodden, R. A., Brown, S. E., Galloway, L. M., Mrazek, S., & Noy, L. (2005, January). *Essential tools: Interagency transition team development and facilitation*. Minneapolis: University of Minnesota College of Education & Human Development. Retrieved from http://www.ncset.org/publications/essential-tools/teams/

Stodden, R. A., & Dowrick, P. W. (2000). The present and future of postsecondary education for adults with disabilities. *Impact, 13*(1), 4–5.

Test, D. W., Fowler, C. H., Richter, S. M., White, J., Mazzotti, V., Walker, A. R., & Kortering, L. (2009). Evidence-based practices in secondary transition. *Career Development for Exceptional Individuals, 32*, 115–128. doi:10.1177/0885728809336859

Uditsky, B., & Hughson, E. (2012). Inclusive postsecondary education—An evidence-based moral imperative. *Journal of Policy & Practice in Intellectual Disabilities, 9*, 298–302. doi:10.1111/jppi.12005

U.S. Department of Education, Office of Career, Technical, and Adult Education. (2015, February). *Making skills everyone's business: A call to transform adult learning in the United States*. Retrieved from https://www2.ed.gov/about/offices/list/ovae/pi/AdultEd/making-skills.pdf

U.S. Department of Health and Human Services and U.S. Department of Education. (2015, September 14). *Policy statement on inclusion of children with disabilities in early childhood programs*. Retrieved from https://www2.ed.gov/policy/speced/guid/earlylearning/joint-statement-full-text.pdf

Yamamoto, K. K., Stodden, R. A., & Folk, E. D. (2014). Inclusive postsecondary education: Reimagining the transition trajectories of vocational rehabilitation clients with intellectual disabilities. *Journal of Vocational Rehabilitation, 40*, 59–71.

CHAPTER 6
Preparing Students for Employment
Kathryn K. Yamamoto, Nancy Farnon-Molfenter, and Evan Nakatsuka

Objectives:
- Introduce key concepts regarding the employment of youth with disabilities.
- Describe central collaborators who provide employment services and who should be included in the planning and service provision process.
- Provide an overview of evidence-based strategies and best practices that promote and support competitive integrated employment outcomes for students with disabilities.

This chapter focuses on preparing transition-age youth with developmental disabilities, including those with autism spectrum disorder and intellectual disability, for employment. Work has been a necessary component of the human existence throughout history. In fact, work has been found to be the central activity in all civilizations and provides the context for fulfilling three basic human needs: (a) survival and power, (b) social connection, and (c) self-determination and well-being (Alsaman & Lee, 2017). Work may be even more beneficial for persons with disabilities who often experience greater social isolation and stigma in combination with higher rates of poverty when compared to their peers without disabilities (Blustein, 2008, as cited in Alsaman & Lee, 2017, p. 98).

Key Terminology	
Competitive integrated employment	Work that provides full- or part-time opportunities (including self-employment), compensates performance at least at minimum wage and equal to peers without disabilities, presents opportunities for advancement comparable to employees in similar positions, and occurs in a setting where the individual interacts with persons who do not have disabilities. (See 29 U.S.C. § 701.)
Customized employment	Work designed to meet both the specific abilities of the individual with a disability and the business needs of the employer. This is accomplished through job exploration and by the person with a disability (and his or her vocational rehabilitation counselor) working with an employer to facilitate an employment match by customizing a job description, work duties, and schedule. (See 29 U.S.C. § 705[7] and 709[c].)
Vocational rehabilitation	A multiprofessional approach to optimizing work participation provided to working-age individuals who have disabilities, limitations, or restrictions with work functioning (Escorpizo et al., 2011, p. 130).

Over the past 40 years, federal legislation such as the Rehabilitation Act of 1973 (2009), the Americans With Disabilities Act of 1990, the School to-Work Opportunity Act of 1994, the Workforce Investment Act of 1998 (superseded by the Workforce Innovation and Opportunity Act of 2014 [WIOA]), and the Ticket to Work and Work Incentives Improvement Act of 1999 have focused on providing opportunities for individuals with disabilities to develop viable work skills and access employment opportunities.

In particular, WIOA (2014) was designed to help job seekers access employment, education, training, and support services to succeed in the labor market and match employers with needed skilled workers. The legislation outlines five categories of pre-employment transition services to be provided collaboratively to students by schools and vocational rehabilitation (VR) services: (a) career counseling, (b) work-based learning, (c) counseling on postsecondary options, (d) workplace readiness and independent living, and (e) self-advocacy. WIOA explicitly states that each state's VR agency must spend 15% of its total allotted funding for services on students with disabilities, while also making clear that school responsibilities for transition planning and services under the Individuals With Disabilities Education

Act (IDEA) remain in place. WIOA places particular emphasis on the need for school and VR services to support individuals with more significant disabilities to achieve this goal by including the requirement for VR to fund customized employment, a service that facilitates job matches to specific skills that are aligned with local employer needs. Thus, a primary intent of WIOA is to provide more robust transition services and collaboration with VR and adult service agencies to improve employment outcomes for individuals with disabilities (Honeycutt, Martin, & Wittenburg, 2017).

In spite of these legislative efforts, research has found that youth with disabilities have poor employment outcomes upon leaving high school (Alsaman & Lee, 2017; Gormley, 2015; Grigal & Hart, 2013; Hendricks, 2010; McDaniels, 2016). In fact, according to the National Longitudinal Transition Study-2 (NLTS2), only 67% of young adults with disabilities who had been out of high school for 8 years obtained full-time employment. In addition, the competitive integrated employment rates for individuals with autism spectrum disorder (ASD) and intellectual disability (ID) were substantially lower than their peers with other disabilities (Newman et al., 2011).

Unfortunately, opportunities for students with disabilities to participate in work experiences during high school vary widely. Such opportunities may be based on whether the student is on a diploma versus certificate track, whether state and local education agencies embrace work-based experiences, and if strong collaboration exists between schools, VR agencies, and adult service partners (Luecking & Luecking, 2015).

Young adults with developmental disabilities including ASD and ID have lower rates of employment (Grigal & Hart, 2013; Oswald, Flexer, Alderman, & Huber, 2016) and earn less than both their peers without disabilities and those with other types of disabilities. Although the transition goals for 78% of high school students with ID and 65% of students with ASD cite the objective of "work in the community" (Gilson & Carter, 2016; Shogren & Plotner, 2012), studies of postschool outcomes reveal that fewer than 40% actually achieve that goal (Gilson & Carter, 2016; Newman et al., 2011). Specifically, the NTLS2 Wave 5 survey of more than 9,000 young adults across all disability categories revealed that fewer than 39% of young adults with ID and only slightly more than 37% with ASD were employed, representing a striking disparity in employment outcomes for these youth (Newman et al., 2011).

Another critical employment issue for this demographic is wage disparity. Employed individuals with ASD and ID typically work in entry-level positions and earn significantly less money than individuals with other disabilities (Ohl et al., 2016; Roux et al., 2013). The wages of former students with ID and ASD averaged approximately $3.00 per hour lower than their peers with other types of disabilities (Newman et al., 2011), due in part to working in segregated settings, holding menial jobs, and working fewer hours (Gilson & Carter, 2016; Kirby, 2016; Roux et al., 2013). In addition, the majority of individuals with ID who work competitively lack basic benefits, including health insurance (Boeltzig et al., 2008; Heyman, Stokes, & Siperstein, 2017).

Barriers to Employment

Youth with disabilities face multiple challenges in the pursuit and retention of employment. For example, teachers and VR counselors cite concerns about behavioral issues for some of this population as a reason to limit or avoid community work experiences (Carter et al., 2013). Many youth with disabilities have not been afforded the chance to develop expected behaviors and emotional regulation skills needed to be considered good candidates for the community work experiences that are critical to being successfully employed after high school. Competency for active participation in life after school stems from planning and supports executed at an early age (Carter et al., 2016). For transitioning youth with disabilities, a lack of context and experience with workplace culture presents challenges with obtaining and maintaining employment. Additional barriers to employment include segregation, attitudes, literacy, and disability characteristics.

Segregation and pervasive low expectations for youth with disabilities affect education and employment settings, create barriers to employment, and contribute to poor employment outcomes (Wehman et al., 2015). Segregation from peers without disabilities leads to hindered development of academic, social, and emotional skills (Carter et al., 2013; Shogren, McCart, Lyon, & Sailor, 2015). Essentially, segregation leads to expectation gaps and perceived skill deficits that affect the career exploration and community work experiences that are critical during the transition years for postschool employment success.

Among the most daunting barriers to employment are societal stigma and negative perceptions about the capabilities of individuals with disabilities (Gormley, 2015; Hendricks, 2010). Attitudinal barriers exist, such as co-workers who may view the hiring of a person with disabilities as unfair due to the job accommodations or additional support that the employee receives. Misperceptions may also lead to unsubstantiated beliefs about high rates of absenteeism, inefficiency, or unforeseen costs to the employer. The legacy of stigma persists and has prompted advocacy efforts through federal legislation (Gormley, 2015).

Often, youth with disabilities require support both in the job-seeking process and later with learning specific job tasks. Limited literacy, numerical, and computer proficiency can serve as barriers to employment. For example, literacy can affect how a person searches for job openings and completes application forms (Lorenz,

Frischling, Cuadros, & Heinitz, 2016; Smith et al., 2015). In addition, both clear written explanations of job responsibilities and unwritten rules (e.g., basic sanitation procedures, chain of command) may need to be directly explained to an employee with a disability.

For individuals with disabilities such as ASD, the lack of social context and atypical behaviors can cause barriers to employment and make the interview process problematic (Lorenz et al. 2016; Smith et al. 2015). Interpersonal interactions and social communication challenges may negatively affect a person with ASD's success after attaining employment. For example, an employee with ASD may experience difficulty in understanding unwritten rules and nonverbal cues, and in following social norms on the job. Individuals with ASD may experience sensory challenges as well, and the sensitivity to stimuli or noises may create anxiety for a worker with ASD. Adapting to changes beyond specific job tasks and stress on the job may lead to behaviors such as pronounced outward displays of frustration or ritualistic behaviors that may create discomfort for others at the workplace (Hendricks, 2010).

Predictors of Positive Employment Outcomes

Establishing integrated competitive employment as the expectation for youth with disabilities and delivering transition services designed for that specific purpose assists individuals to secure and maintain jobs in their communities (Luecking, 2009; Schall et al., 2015). Understanding the in-school predictors of postschool success in this transition domain can shed light on best practices that have been underutilized for the majority of youth with disabilities (Cobb, Lipscomb, Wolgemuth, & Schulte, 2013; Mazzotti, Test, & Mustian, 2014). As discussed in Chapter 5, research has attested that inclusion in general education classes can contribute to a student's postschool success (Kurth, Lyon, & Shogren, 2015; Mazzotti et al., 2016; Odom, Buysse, & Soukakou, 2011). Research has also demonstrated that the development of social and self-determination skills, parent involvement, expectations for employment, and participation in direct work experience (including the provision of VR services) contribute to postschool success (Burgess & Cimera, 2014; Carter, Austin, & Trainor, 2012; Chen, Sung, & Pi, 2015; Honeycutt, Thompkins, Bardos, & Stern, 2014; Luecking & Luecking, 2015; Shogren & Plotner, 2012; Test et al., 2009; Wehman et al., 2015). These research findings provide the foundation for the model in Figure 6.1 depicting specific predictors that lead to positive employment outcomes for youth with disabilities. This model in turn serves as the foundation for the following recommendations of evidence-based practices and strategies educators may use with youth with disabilities.

Figure. 6.1. Predictors of Positive Employment Outcomes

Collaboration

Collaboration among student, family, special educators, and adult service providers enhances the transition process and future outlook.

High expectations

All involved parties set high postsecondary expectations.

Inclusion

Greater inclusion throughout school years and being in classes alongside peers affords students the opportunity to attain successful transition outcomes.

Self-determination

Learning to communicate strengths, interests, and needs during the transition process is integral to preparing for employment.

Individualized career goals

Students who are directly involved in setting employment goals based on their preferences, interests, and strengths are more likely to live productive lives.

Community work experiences

Promote high quality work experiences while student is still in high school.

Competitive integrated employment

Support work opportunities that are performed in integrated settings, compensated at least at minimum wage, and present advancement opportunities equal to peers without disabilities.

Collaboration

Recommendation: Invite key collaborators such as VR counselors and other adult service providers to individualized education program meetings to discuss with the individual with the disability, the family, and other members of the educational team how these services may address the student's needs. Research is clear that collaboration with other professionals in the field will enhance the transition process and future outlook for students with disabilities (Nicholas et al., 2017). If the student is eligible for services, agencies can also commit resources to pay for or provide needed transition services (U.S. Department of Education, 2000). Table 6.1 provides an overview of key agencies that can support students with disabilities in their quest toward employment, self-sufficiency, and independence.

High Expectations

Recommendation: Set high expectations! Go beyond the status quo and avoid stereotypic, "cookie-cutter" employment goals and work experiences. Develop career and technical education courses that represent a wide variety of occupations, to provide opportunities for choice that matches students' preferences, interests, needs, and strengths (Rowe et al., 2015). Ensure students have the opportunity to be in classes alongside their typically developing peers. This inclusion raises postschool employment expectations and affords students the opportunity to attain knowledge, work skills, and social skills (Molfenter & Hanley-Maxwell, 2017; Test, Smith, & Carter, 2014).

Inclusion

Recommendation: Provide opportunities for youth with disabilities to be included in general education classes and extracurricular activities alongside peers without disabilities. This inclusion has been shown to assist youth with disabilities in achieving more successful transition outcomes, including employment (McConnell, Martin, & Hennessey, 2015). In order to support meaningful high school inclusion, teachers can use strategies such as opportunity or community mapping (discussed in Chapter 8) or person-centered planning (discussed in Chapter 4) processes to get students involved in classes and activities that are aligned with postschool goals and interests (Swedeen, Carter, & Molfenter, 2010). Teachers may also implement co-teaching, universal design for learning, and peer support arrangements to facilitate inclusion. (For more ideas on ways to increase high school inclusion, visit Wisconsin's Let's Get to Work website at http://www.letsgettoworkwi.org.)

Table 6.1. Support Agencies' Roles in Transition to Employment		
Agency	**Role**	**Resources**
State Vocational Rehabilitation (VR)	Assists eligible individuals with disabilities to assess, plan, develop, and access services for the purpose of preparing for and engaging in employment	Rehabilitation Services Administration, Frequently Asked Questions web page: https://rsa.ed.gov/faqs.cfm#employed
State Medicaid Agency Social Security Administration	Provides long-term supports to individuals with significant disabilities; adult services can begin at age 18 (recommendation is to apply for services before age 18)	Medicaid Employment Initiatives web page: https://www.medicaid.gov/medicaid/ltss/employmment/index.html Social Security Administration "Working While Disabled—How We Can Help"; available at https://www.ssa.gov/pubs/ Social Security Administration, "Compilation of the Social Security Laws" web page: https://www.ssa.gov/OP_Home/ssact/title19/1915.htm
Departments of Education and Labor	Provide guidance for state and local workforce development systems that increase the skill and credential attainment, employment, retention, and earnings of participants, especially those with significant barriers to employment	Workforce Innnovation and Opportunity Act Final Rule web page: https://www.doleta.gov/wioa/Docs/wioa-regs-joint-final-rule.pdf
Community rehabilitation program (CRP)	Provides employment support services; youth with disabilities may receive transition services from school staff, become a VR consumer, and receive additional services through a CRP	USLegal website's definition of CRP: https://definitions.uslegal.com/c/community-rehabilitation-program/

Self-Determination

Recommendation: Teach youth with disabilities to communicate their strengths, interests, and needs during the transition process, as this is integral to preparing for employment (Martin & Williams-Diehm, 2013; McDougall, Evans, & Baldwin, 2010). This is referred to as *self-determination*, which is defined as having the ability, motivation, and support needed to direct one's own life in ways and a direction that are personally meaningful (Carter, Trainor, Cakiroglu, Swedeen, & Owens, 2010). Special educators should provide youth with disabilities with many opportunities to communicate and collaborate with others and to make decisions about their future.

Students should learn about both their strengths and their challenges (i.e., disability) and the accommodations and modifications they require to learn in the adult world. With this knowledge, students can practice informing professionals (e.g., teachers, employers, disability services office) of their academic and learning needs. This will help them secure individualized support required for optimal success in a variety of settings. Teachers can use available resources such as lesson plans (e.g., the University of Oklahoma's Zarrow Center for Learning Enrichment's transition education materials; Wisconsin Department of Public Instruction's transition planning lesson plans) and mobile applications (apps; e.g., iTransition, WiTransition) designed to capture student and family input and foster self-direction in the transition planning process.

Individualized Career Goals

Recommendation: Help youth with disabilities develop individualized postschool career and employment goals based on their preferences, interests, needs, and strengths (Martin & Williams-Diehm, 2013). The use of individualized learning plans and the academic career planning process are gaining recognition as ways of engaging students in career exploration and goal setting (Solberg, Phelps, Haakenson, Durham, & Timmons, 2012). Students who are directly involved in setting employment goals are more likely to pursue interests and ultimately live productive lives (Camacho & Hemmeter, 2013). Camacho and Hemmeter (2013) advocated a person-centered approach to transition planning, which should include discussion about current and future employment. Educating students with disabilities about how to set appropriate employment goals takes place through involvement in the transition planning process and balancing desired outcomes with skills and abilities (Balcazar et al., 2012). A person-centered approach to transition planning should also include a team composed of individuals with different areas of expertise, including those with vocational backgrounds. As illustrated in Figure 6.2, the student should be the center of discussion and decision making. In this model, students learn about resources and supports and are able to make informed decisions regarding their future (including their career) through collaboration with the transition planning team.

In Table 6.2, we provide strategies to facilitate individualized experiential assessment and learning that teachers may incorporate into their daily classroom activities to help students create individualized career goals.

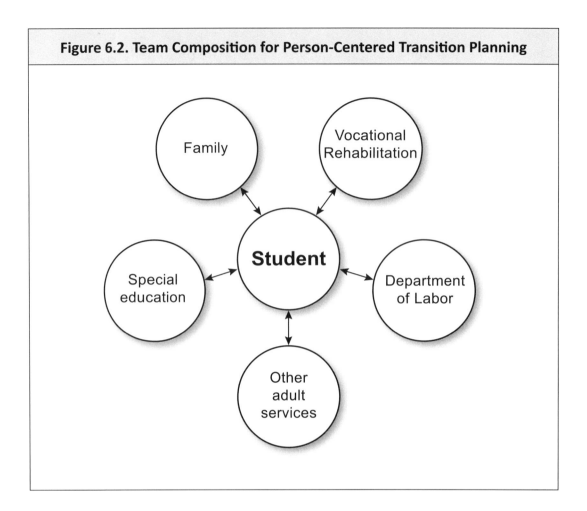

Figure 6.2. Team Composition for Person-Centered Transition Planning

Community Work Experiences

Recommendation: Provide opportunities for students with disabilities to participate in direct community work experiences during high school. These opportunities can assist individuals with disabilities to become and remain competitively employed in integrated work settings (Mazzotti et al., 2016; Wehman et al., 2015). Educators should promote high quality, on-the-job work experiences (job-shadowing, community service learning, work-study, school-based enterprises, apprenticeships, internships). Opportunities can begin with unpaid, exploratory experiences with the ultimate goal of paid integrated employment (Datson et al., 2012; Wehman et al., 2014).

Table 6.2. Strategies to Facilitate Individualized Experiential Assessment and Learning

Strategies	Resources
Observe and note what the student enjoys and does well in school setting (e.g., preferred subjects, environments, best times of day, peers, down time).	Hagner, 2010
Ask the student, family members, and others who know the student well about favorite places, activities, and nonnegotiables (i.e., important things).	Wehman et al., 2012
Arrange for the student to spend time helping with tasks in the school building or district (e.g., school store, library, cafeteria, office, early childhood program).	Smith, Dillahunt-Aspillaga, & Kenney, 2017
Conduct "intentional hanging out" to discover places, activities, people, and environments that are a good fit for the student.	Hagner, 2010
Incorporate community-based instruction, job shadowing, and internships as part of the special education curriculum.	Solberg, Phelps, Haakenson, Durham, & Timmons, 2012
Document activities while the student is in high school (including volunteerism) and contact information of supports and references within the community.	Datson, Riehle, & Rutkowski, 2012
Coordinate and participate in person-centered planning to focus on informed choice, self-advocacy, and self-direction of transition services.	Martin & Williams-Diehm, 2013
Communicate with VR counselors/educational coaches to inform them of student's priorities and work preferences; share assessment results, work discovery notes, job seeker profiles, and work experiences with VR with the consent of the student/parents.	Migliore, Timmons, Butterworth, & Lugas, 2012
Identify online resources to facilitate the process.	Let's Get to Work, http://www.letsgettoworkwi.org/

Note. VR = vocational rehabilitation.

Competitive Integrated Employment

Recommendation: Provide supported employment opportunities, on-the-job training, and long-term supports to meet the goal of competitive integrated employment for individuals with disabilities. Supported employment is an intervention model designed to assist people with significant disabilities to gain and maintain competitive integrated employment. One of the main aspects of supported employment is to provide individualized supports to supplement the general onboarding and training procedures of an employer so that a new employee with a disability can integrate into the workplace and learn the skills necessary to perform the expected duties.

Customized employment is an approach recognized as an option of the supported employment model under WIOA (Riesen, Morgan, & Griffin, 2015). This approach is designed to match an employer's identified needs with the unique skills and strengths of an individual with a disability as determined through experiential assessment (Smith et al., 2017). The customized employment model focuses on creating a mutually beneficial relationship between an employee with a disability and employer by creating a job opportunity that utilizes the talents of the employee to address the unmet operational demands of the employer (Riesen et al., 2015).

On-the-job training is a needed support once a job seeker with a disability secures competitive integrated employment. This skills training can help an individual master specific job tasks, build independence, and integrate into the workplace (Gilson & Carter, 2016). The goal of on-the-job training is to foster independence and fade on-site support.

Long-term supports are designed to monitor job satisfaction, assist with communicating the worker's needs and role during turnover of supervisors or other key co-workers, provide additional job coaching when changes in company policies impact job performance, and assist in the pursuit of opportunities for advancement. These supports focus on job retention and navigating changes in the workplace (Brooke, Revell, & Wehman, 2009). A young adult may require long-term supports from adult service providers or natural supports such as co-workers, which can be essential components of a long-term successful employment outcome (Brooke et al., 2009).

Summary

The explicit goal of preschool-to-Grade 12 education for all students, including those who receive special education services, is to graduate from high school ready to accomplish postschool goals, obtain employment, and achieve self-sufficiency (Bebell & Stemler, 2013). Available data on employment outcomes for youth with disabilities demonstrate the need for more targeted and consistent educational supports to prepare for competitive integrated employment (Luecking & Luecking, 2015; Simonsen & Neubert, 2013). In order to successfully venture from the role of "student" to that of "contributing member of society," these youth must learn about their strengths and challenges in relation to the world of work; understand employer–employee relationships and responsibilities; and develop marketable skills, by actively participating in work-related and competitive work experiences before exiting high school. Special educators and other practitioners in the field would benefit from understanding the vast array of employment-focused models and best practices and embrace the challenge of incorporating these into their curricula. By better understanding the roles of adult service providers (Luecking, 2009) and the strategies that support integrated competitive employment, special educators can prepare youth with disabilities to advocate for and utilize appropriate resources; collaborate more effectively; and proceed toward a positive trajectory to adulthood, independence, and employment.

References

Alsaman, M. A., & Lee, C. L. (2017). Employment outcomes for youth with disabilities in vocational rehabilitation: A multilevel analysis of RSA-911 data. *Rehabilitation Counseling Bulletin, 60*, 98–107. doi:10.1177/003455216632363

Balcazar, F. E., Taylor-Ritzler, T., Dimpfl, S., Portillo-Peña, N., Guzman, A., Schiff, R., & Murvay, M. (2012). Improving the transition outcomes of low-income minority youth with disabilities. *Exceptionality, 20*, 114–132. doi:10.1080/09362835.2012.670599

Bebell, D., & Stemler, S. (2013). *The school mission statement: Values, goals, and identities in American education*. New York, NY: Routledge.

Blustein, D. L. (2008). The role of work in psychological health and well-being. *American Psychologist, 63*, 228–240. doi:10.1037/0003-066X.63.4.228

Boeltzig, H., Timmons, J. C., & Butterworth, J. (2008). Entering work: Employment outcomes of people with developmental disabilities. *International Journal of Rehabilitation Research, 31*, 217-223. doi:10.1097/MRR.0b013e3282fb7ce5

Brooke, V., Revell G., & Wehman, P. (2009). Quality indicators for competitive employment outcomes: What special education teachers need to know in transition planning. *TEACHING Exceptional Children, 41*(4), 58–66. doi:10.1177/004005990904100406

Burgess, S., & Cimera, R. E. (2014). Employment outcomes of transition-aged adults with autism spectrum disorders: A state of the states report. *American Journal on Intellectual and Developmental Disabilities, 119*, 64–83. doi:10.1352/1944-7558-119.1.64

Camacho, C. B., & Hemmeter, J. (2013). Linking youth transition support services: Results from two demonstration projects. *Social Security Bulletin, 73*(1), 59.

Carter, E. W., Asmus, J., Moss, C. K., Biggs, E. E., Bolt, D. M., Born, T. L., & Fesperman, E. (2016). Randomized evaluation of peer support arrangements to support the inclusion of high school students with severe disabilities. *Exceptional Children, 82*, 209–233. doi:10.1177/0014402915598780

Carter, E. W., Austin, D., & Trainor, A. A. (2012). Predictors of postschool employment outcomes for young adults with severe disabilities. *Journal of Disability Policy Studies, 23*, 50–63. doi:10.1177/1044207311414680

Carter, E. W., Lane, K. L., Cooney, M., Weir, K., Moss, C. K., & Machalicek, W. (2013). Determination among transition-age youth with autism or intellectual disability: Parent perspectives. *Research and Practice for Persons with Severe Disabilities, 38*, 129–138. doi:10.1177/154079691303800301

Carter, E. W., Trainor, A. A., Cakiroglu, O., Swedeen, B., & Owens, L. A. (2010). Availability of and access to career development activities for transition-age youth with disabilities. *Career Development for Exceptional Individuals, 33*, 13–24. doi:10.1177/0885728809344332

Chen, J. L., Sung, C., & Pi, S. (2015). Vocational rehabilitation service patterns and outcomes for individuals with autism of different ages. *Journal of Autism and Developmental Disorders, 45*, 3015–3029. doi:10.1007/s10803-015-2465-y

Cobb, R. B., Lipscomb, S., Wolgemuth, J., & Schulte, T. (2013, August). *Improving post-high school outcomes for transition-age students with disabilities: An evidence review* (NCEE 2013-4011). Washington, DC: U.S. Department of Education, Institute of Education Sciences. Retrieved from https://files.eric.ed.gov/fulltext/ED544172.pdf

Datson M., Riehle J. E., Rutkowski S. (2012). *High school transition that works: Lessons learned from Project Search*. Baltimore, MD: Paul H. Brookes.

Escorpizo, R., Reneman, M. F., Ekholm, J., Fritz, J., Krupa, T., Marnetoft, S. U., ... Chann, C. C. (2011). A conceptual definition of vocational rehabilitation based on ICF: Building a shared global model. *Journal of Occupational Rehabilitation, 21*, 126–133. doi:10.1007/10926-011-9292-6

Gilson, C., & Carter, E. (2016). Promoting social interactions and job independence for college students with autism or intellectual disability: A pilot study. *Journal of Autism & Developmental Disabilities, 46*, 3583–3596. doi:10.1007/s10803-016-2894-2

Gormley, M. E., (2015). Workplace stigma toward employees with intellectual disability: A descriptive study. *Journal of Vocational Rehabilitation, 43*, 249–258. doi:10.3233/JVR-150773

Grigal, M., & Hart, D. (2013). Transition and postsecondary education programs for students with intellectual disability: A pathway to employment. *Think College! Fast Facts, 4*. Boston: University of Massachusetts Boston, Institute for Community Inclusion.

Hagner, D. (2010). The role of naturalistic assessment in vocational rehabilitation. *Journal of Rehabilitation, 76*(1), 28–34.

Hendricks, D. (2010). Employment and adults with autism spectrum disorders: Challenges and strategies for success. *Journal of Vocational Rehabilitation, 32*, 125–134. doi:10.32233/JVR-2010-0502.

Heyman, M., Stokes, J. E., & Siperstein, G. N. (2017). Not all jobs are the same: Predictors of job quality for adults with intellectual disabilities. *Journal of Vocational Rehabilitation, 44*, 299–306. doi:10.3233/JVR-160800

Honeycutt, T., Martin, F., & Wittenburg, D. (2017). Transitions and vocational rehabilitation success: Tracking outcomes for different types of youth. *Journal of Vocational Rehabilitation, 46*, 137–148. doi:10.3233/JVR-160850

Honeycutt, T., Thompkins, A., Bardos, M., & Stern, S. (2014). State differences in the vocational rehabilitation experiences of transition-age youth with disabilities. *Journal of Vocational Rehabilitation, 42*, 17–30. doi:10.3233/JVR-140721

Kirby, A. V. (2016). Parent expectations mediate outcomes for young adults with autism spectrum disorder. Journal of *Autism and Developmental Disorders, 46*, 1643–1655. doi:10.1007/s10803-015-2691-3

Kurth, J. A., Lyon, K. J., & Shogren, K. A. (2015). Supporting students with severe disabilities in inclusive schools. *Research & Practice for Persons with Severe Disabilities, 40*, 261–274. doi:10.1177/1540796915594160

Lorenz, T., Frischling, C., Cuadros, R., & Heinitz, K. (2016). Autism and overcoming job barriers: Comparing job-related barriers and possible solutions in and outside of autism-specific employment. *PLOS ONE, 11*(1), 1–19. doi:10.1371/journal.pone.0147040

Luecking, D. M., & Luecking, R. G. (2015). Translating research into a seamless transition model. *Career Development and Transition for Exceptional Individuals, 38*, 4–13. doi:10.1177/2165143413508978

Luecking, R. G. (2009). *The way to work: How to facilitate work experiences for youth in transition*. Baltimore, MD: Paul H. Brookes.

Martin, J. E., & Williams-Diehm, K. (2013). Student engagement and leadership of the transition planning process. *Career Development and Transition for Exceptional Individuals, 36*, 43–50. doi:10.1177/21651434313476545

Mazzotti, V. L., Rowe, D. A., Sinclair, J., Poppen, M., Woods, W. E., & Shearer, M. L. (2016). Predictors of postschool success: A systematic review of the NLTS2 secondary analyses. *Career Development and Transition for Exceptional Individuals, 39*, 196–215. doi:10.1177/2165143415588047

Mazzotti, V. L., Test, D. W., & Mustian, A. L. (2014). Secondary transition evidence-based practices and predictors: Implications for policymakers. *Journal of Disability Policy Studies, 25*, 5–18. doi:10.1177/1044207312460888

McConnell, A. E., Martin, J. E., & Hennessey, M. N. (2015). Indicators of postsecondary employment and education for youth with disabilities in relation to GPA and general education. *Remedial and Special Education, 36*, 327–336. doi:10.1177/0741932515583497

McDaniels, B. (2016). Disproportionate opportunities: Fostering vocational choice for individuals with intellectual disabilities. *Journal of Vocational Rehabilitation, 45*, 19–26. doi:10.3233/JVR-160807.

McDougall, J., Evans, J., & Baldwin, P. (2010). The importance of self-determination to perceived quality of life for youth and young adults with chronic conditions and disabilities. *Remedial and Special Education, 31*, 252–260. doi:10.1177/0741932509355989

Migliore, A., Timmons, J., Butterworth, J., & Lugas, J. (2012). Predictors of employment and postsecondary education of youth with autism. *Rehabilitation Counseling Bulletin, 5*, 176–184. doi:10.1177/0034355212438943

Molfenter, N., & Hanley-Maxwell, C. (2017). Ethics of Inclusion for secondary students with intellectual and developmental disabilities in the United States. In C. Forlin & A. Gajewski (Eds.), *Ethics, equity, and inclusive education* (pp. 79–117). Bingley, England: Emerald.

Newman, L., Wagner, M., Knokey, A. M., Marder, C., Nagle, K., Shaver, D., & Wei, X. (2011). *The post-high school outcomes of young adults with disabilities up to 8 Years after high school: A report from the National Longitudinal Transition Study-2* (NLTS2; NCSER 2011-3005). Washington, DC: U.S. Department of Education, Institute of Education Sciences. Retrieved from https://ies.ed.gov/ncser/pubs/20113005/pdf/20113005.pdf

Nicholas, D. B., Hodgetts, S., Zwaigenbaum, L., Smith, L. E., Shattuck, P., Parr, J. R., & Stothers, M. E. (2017). Research needs and priorities for transition and employment in autism: Considerations reflected in a "special interest group" at the International Meeting for Autism Research. *Autism Research, 10*, 15–24. doi:10.1002/aur.1683/full

Odom, S. L., Buysse, V., & Soukakou, E. (2011). Inclusion for young children with disabilities: A quarter century of research perspectives. *Journal of Early Intervention, 33*, 344–356. doi:10.1177/1053815111430094

Ohl, A., Sheff, M. G., Little, S., Nguyen, J., Paskor, K., & Zanjirian, A. (2016). Predictors of employment status among adults with autism spectrum disorder. *Work, 56*, 345–355. doi:10.3233/WOR-172492

Oswald, G., Flexer, R., Alderman, L. A., Huber, M. (2016). Predictive value of personal characteristics and the employment of transition-aged youth in vocational rehabilitation. *Journal of Rehabilitation, 82*(4), 60–66.

Rehabilitation Act of 1973, as amended by Pub. L. No. 110-325, to be codified at 29 U.S.C. § 701 (2009).

Riesen, T., Morgan, R. L., & Griffin, C. (2015). Customized employment: A review of the literature. *Journal of Vocational Rehabilitation, 43*, 183–193. doi:10.3233/JVR150768

Roux, A. M., Shattuck, P. T., Cooper, B. P., Anderson, K. A., Wagner, M., & Narendorf, S. C. (2013). Postsecondary employment experiences among young adults with an autism spectrum disorder. *Journal of the American Academy of Child and Adolescent Psychiatry, 52*, 931–939. doi: 10.1016/j.jaac.2013.05.019.

Rowe, D. A., Alverson, C. Y., Unruh, D. K., Fowler, C. H., Kellems, R., & Test, D. W. (2015). A Delphi study to operationalize evidence-based predictors in secondary transition. *Career Development and Transition for Exceptional Individuals, 38*, 113–126. doi:10:1177/2165143414526429

Schall, C. M., Wehman, P., Brooke, V., Graham, C., McDonough, J., Brooke, A., & Allen, J. (2015). Employment interventions for individuals with ASD: The relative efficacy of supported employment with or without prior Project SEARCH training. *Journal of Autism and Developmental Disorders, 45*, 3990–4001. doi:10.1007/s10803-015-2426-5

Shogren, K. A., McCart, A. B., Lyon, K. J., & Sailor, W. S. (2015). All means all: Building knowledge for inclusive schoolwide transformation. *Research and Practice for Persons with Severe Disabilities, 40*, 173–191. doi:10.1177/154076796915586191

Shogren, K. A., & Plotner, A. J. (2012). Transition planning for students with intellectual disability, autism, or other disabilities: Data from the National Longitudinal Transition Study-2. *Intellectual and Developmental Disabilities, 50*, 16–30. doi:10.1352/1934-9556-50.1.16?code=aamr-site

Simonsen, M. L., & Neubert, D. A. (2013). Transitioning youth with intellectual and other developmental disabilities: Predicting community employment outcomes. *Career Development and Transition for Exceptional Individuals, 36*, 188–198. doi:10.1177/21651443412469399

Smith, M. J., Fleming, M. F., Wright, M. A., Losh, M., Humm, L. B., Olsen, D., & Bell M. D. (2015). Brief report: Vocational outcomes for young adults with autism spectrum disorders at six months after virtual reality job interview training. *Journal of Autism & Developmental Disorders, 45*, 3364–3369. doi:10.1007/s10803-015-2470-1

Smith, T. J., Dillahunt-Aspillaga, C. J., & Kenney, R. M. (2017). Implementation of customized employment provisions of the Workforce Innovation and Opportunity Act within vocational rehabilitation systems. *Journal of Disability Policy Studies, 27*, 195–202. doi:10.1177/10442073166444412

Solberg, V. S., Phelps, L. A., Haakenson, K. A., Durham, J. F., & Timmons, J. (2012). The nature and use of individualized learning plans as a promising career intervention strategy. *Journal of Career Development, 39*, 500–514. doi:10.1177/0894845311414571

Swedeen, B. L., Carter, E. W., & Molfenter, N. (2010). Getting everyone involved: Identifying transition opportunities for youth with severe disabilities. *TEACHING Exceptional Children, 43*(2), 38–49. doi:10.1177/004005991004300204

Test, D. W., Mazzotti, V. L., Mustian, A. L., Fowler, C. H., Kortering, L., & Kohler, P. (2009). Evidence-based secondary transition predictors for improving postschool outcomes for students with disabilities. *Career Development for Exceptional Individuals, 32*, 160–181. doi:10.1177/0885728809346960

Test, D. W., Smith, L. E., & Carter, E. W. (2014). Equipping youth with autism spectrum disorders for adulthood: Promoting rigor, relevance, and relationships. *Remedial and Special Education, 35*, 80–90. doi:10.1177/0741932513514857

U.S. Department of Education, Office of Special Education and Rehabilitative Services. (2000, July). *A guide to the individualized education program.* Retrieved from https://www2.ed.gov/parents/needs/speced/iepguide/index.html#team

Wehman, P., Lau, S., Molinelli, A., Brooke, V., Thompson, K., Moore, C., & West, M. (2012). Supported employment for young adults with autism spectrum disorder: Preliminary data. *Research & Practice for Persons with Severe Disabilities, 37*, 160–169. doi:10.2511/027494812804153606

Wehman, P., Schall, C., Carr, S., Targett, P., West, M., & Cifu, G. (2014). Transition from school to adulthood for youth with autism spectrum disorder: What we know and what we need to know. *Journal of Disability Policy Studies, 25*, 30–40. doi:10.1177/1044207313518071

Wehman, P., Sima, A. P., Ketchum, J., West, M. D., Chan, F., & Luecking, R. (2015). Predictors of successful transition from school to employment for youth with disabilities. *Journal of Occupational Rehabilitation, 25*, 323–334. doi:10.1007/s10926-014-9541-6

Workforce Innovation and Opportunity Act, 29 U.S.C. Ch. 32 (2014).

CHAPTER 7
Preparing Students for Postsecondary Education
L. Lynn Stansberry Brusnahan, Marc Ellison, and Dedra Hafner

Objectives
- Outline the benefits of postsecondary higher education for students with disabilities.
- Present two higher education models for inclusion of students with disabilities.
- Discuss barriers to higher education success, both institutional and directly related to disability characteristics.
- Highlight effective practices that prepare students for postsecondary education settings while they are still in high school.
- Highlight effective practices to meet the needs of students with disabilities in postsecondary education settings.

This chapter focuses on the topic of postsecondary education (PSE) for youth with developmental disabilities, including those with autism spectrum disorder and intellectual disability (ID). In the postsecondary setting, students who previously received special education support under the Individuals With Disabilities Education Act (IDEA, 2006) can be covered by the civil rights protections of Section 504 of the Rehabilitation Act of 1973 (2009) and the Americans With Disabilities Act (1990; ADA Amendments Act [ADAAA], 2009). Whereas the IDEA mandates a free and appropriate public education (FAPE), the ADA and Section 504 protect against discrimination and ensure students accessibility (Griffin & Papay, 2017; Madaus & Shaw, 2004). Per Section 504, qualified individuals may not be denied or subjected to discrimination in admission or excluded from participation in activities such as academics, athletics, recreation, or other extracurricular activities on the basis of a disability (Connor; 2012; Zager & Smith, 2012). The ADAAA protects individuals with disabilities against discrimination in postsecondary education settings by requiring access to reasonable accommodations, but does not require modifications that would alter fundamental requirements of an academic course.

Key Terminology	
Postsecondary education	Education after high school at institutes of higher education (i.e., colleges or universities offering degrees), technical, vocational, and community colleges.
Office of Postsecondary Education (OPE)	The U.S. Department of Education's OPE is dedicated to strengthening colleges and universities capacity to reform, innovate, and improve postsecondary education; promote and expand access to postsecondary education; increase completion rates; and broaden competencies for economic success.
Transition and Postsecondary Programs for Students with Intellectual Disabilities (TPSID)	TPSID projects, funded by the U.S. Department of Education, provide institutions of higher education grant funding to create or expand inclusive model comprehensive transition and postsecondary programs for students with intellectual disability.
Think College	The goal of this national organization is to develop, expand, and improve inclusive higher education options for people with intellectual disability. One way this organization works to meet this goal is by generating and sharing knowledge with students, professionals, and families.

The higher education environment offers individuals with disabilities opportunities to gain knowledge and skills they may not have had access to in high school (Hartz, 2014; Moon, Grigal, & Neubert, 2001; Uditsky & Hughson, 2012). Although some individuals with autism spectrum disorder have the academic ability to meet traditional entrance criteria, other individuals with developmental disabilities may have difficulty being accepted and accessing services in the postsecondary environment (Grigal & Hart, 2010; Hartz, 2014). To address this challenge, the U.S. Department of Education's Office of Postsecondary Education supported the creation of Transition and Postsecondary Programs for Students With Intellectual Disabilities (TPSID) (Grigal, Hart, Smith, Domin, & Weir, 2017). The Think College website (https://thinkcollege.net) lists the TPSID and other inclusive college programs across the United States dedicated to PSE for students with intellectual and developmental disabilities. These inclusive programs provide pathways to participation that historically have not been available to students with some disabilities due to the constraints of the traditional requirements of a high school diploma, grade point average, or entrance examination test scores (Griffin & Papay, 2017; Grigal, Hart, & Weir, 2012).

Benefits of Postsecondary Education

PSE offers opportunities and resources to students with disabilities that can facilitate and maintain improved quality of life (Hart, Grigal, & Weir, 2010). The benefits of participation in higher education for individuals with disabilities can be measured not just academically, but also relative to student growth in personal skills (Griffin & Papay, 2017). Being part of campus life, taking college classes with students without disabilities, and learning to navigate a world of high expectations leads to the development of skills needed for successful adult life and valued roles within society (Hart et al., 2010). Participation in continuing education for individuals with disabilities can provide economic and social benefits and increase independence (Hart et al., 2010).

An economic advantage of completing higher education is that it can lead to enhanced lifetime earnings (Carnevale, Rose, & Cheah, 2011). According to The College Board, PSE can provide more stable employment and job satisfaction contributing to a higher quality of life, including employment at double the rate of those with just a high school diploma (Baum, Ma, & Payea, 2013; Gilmore, Bose, & Hart, 2001).

A second advantage to higher education is the social benefits for students with disabilities. PSE settings provide opportunities for young adults with disabilities to develop a sense of community and belonging through campus clubs and other nonacademic activities that expand networks and involvement with people without disabilities (Grigal, Neubert, & Moon, 2002; Hafner, 2008; Hart, Zimbrich, & Parker, 2005). Participation in PSE increases opportunities to engage with typical peers; having these social role models increases the probability that students with disabilities will continue to participate in a variety of integrated settings throughout their lives (Alper, 2003; Hartz, 2014; Moon et al., 2001; Uditsky & Hughson, 2012).

An advantage to higher education inclusion for all students, with and without disabilities, is that going to college is a natural stepping-stone to learning independent living skills through the demands of campus life (Alwell & Cobb, 2009; Bouck, 2010; Hartz, 2014; Lindstrom, Doren, & Miesch, 2011). Evidence supports the importance of promoting independence skills in students with disabilities. Integrated campus settings provide learning environments offering opportunities for growth that will serve students throughout their lifespan, including self-efficacy, self-determination, self-advocacy, self-confidence, and a sense of identity (Cobb, Lehmann, Newman-Gonchar, & Alwell, 2009; de Araujo

& Murray, 2010; Grigal, Weir, Hart, & Opsal, 2013; Hafner & Moffatt, 2012; Hartz, 2014; Lindstrom et al., 2011; Moon et al., 2001; Uditsky & Hughson, 2012; Wehmeyer et al., 2011).

Non-Traditional Higher Education Options

There are traditional and non-traditional paths in higher education. Non-traditional paths are for students who are not matriculating and who are not pursuing a degree or certificate. In these instances, there are a variety of options that students with disabilities can consider to access PSE (Stansberry Brusnahan, Ellison, & Hafner, 2017). Two models are dual or concurrent enrollment for high school students and college-initiated programs (Hart et al., 2010). (See Table 7.1).

With the dual or concurrent enrollment model, an institute of higher education and local education agency partner to offer a program where transition-age (18–21 years old) students enroll via "special student" status (not related to special education). Students have access to the institution's facilities while they are still technically high school students (Neubert, Moon, Grigal, & Redd, 2002). In this model, students might have options to take a course for audit, credit, non-credit, or continuing education, or participate in a totally separate curriculum designed for students with disabilities that provides individualized supports and services (Hart et al., 2005). Partnerships between colleges and local education agencies can facilitate opportunities for student with disabilities to also participate in extracurricular activities alongside their typical peers. With this model, the school district might consider the college as a "community environment" for teaching functional and foundational skills. The college would provide the staff support and student accommodations under the auspices of the local school district with staff employed by the district. Another approach is for the institution of higher education to provide the transition program for students and build the costs of specialized supports into tuition fees via school-district financing. In some cases, professors or departments have contracts to provide special courses designed to include transition students (Hafner, 2008).

With the college-initiated model, institutions of higher education (sometimes in conjunction with adult service agencies or disability organizations) create programs aimed at providing access and supporting individuals around 18 to 24 years old with disabilities on college campuses. This model views all students as adult learners and provides an inclusive environment that mirrors a typical college experience. This option is typically tuition-based, and offers the same range and diversity of services as for other students, over the course of 2 to 4 years (Hart et al., 2010). With this model, students with disabilities have socially valued roles, created and maintained through participation in the same activities and environments as their peers. This model provides opportunities for students to

Table 7.1. Characteristics of Non-Traditional Postsecondary Education Models

Concurrent enrollment models	College-initiated models
• Provide dual enrollment in the K-12 educational system and PSE for students with disabilities who are between the ages of 18-21 • Provide funding through the LEA's postsecondary program, which can be accomplished in different ways	• Provide access to PSE for students with disabilities • Provide an inclusive environment that mirrors a typical undergraduate IHE experience • Ensure students with disabilities have socially valued roles through participation in the same activities and environments as peers • View IHEs as a natural transition and pathway to the world of work and community involvement for all students • View all students as adult learners • Extend education beyond the classroom and do not limit a student's education to just classroom learning • Plan for success utilizing a person-centered planning focus, which includes support services based on student's preferences and choices • Provide opportunities for students to establish friendships and relationships • Provide individualized services, accommodations, and supports to ensure access and participation for students with disabilities • Matriculate students to work toward completion of a course of study resulting in employment • Provide job training and/or opportunities for internships for students • Design a student-centered program of inclusion where the student's disability is not their defining characteristic • Fund through a collaboration of the IHE, LEA, and the family (Hafner, 2008)

Note. PSE = postsecondary education; LEA = local education agency; IHE = institution of higher education.

establish relationships. It also provides individualized services, accommodations, and supports to ensure access and participation. In this model, there is a student-centered program of inclusion where the student's disability is not his or her defining characteristic. These models are typically funded through a collaboration of the college, local public school district, and the family (Hafner, 2008).

Higher Education Barriers

Students with disabilities can face significant barriers to a successful college outcome. These barriers can be institutional or disability-related, and may present this student population with significant challenges to a successful transition into and completion of their goals within higher education (Stansberry Brusnahan et al., 2017).

Institutional Barriers

Institution barriers can include a lack of support, services, and resources. The demographic of college students with disabilities is relatively new on campus, with fewer than 3% of U.S. college students disclosing a disability in the mid-1970s (Madaus, 2011). A 2014 survey found that fewer than 6% of college students with disabilities self-reported their disability (McGregor et al., 2016).

Traditional mindsets and negative attitudes on college campuses about disability may create a general lack of understanding and unwillingness to provide supports (Ellison, Clark, Cunningham, & Hansen, 2013). Some characteristics of individuals with disabilities can be a source of confusion, and faculty and staff in higher education may be uncertain how to accommodate their needs (Ellison et al., 2013; Farrell, 2004; VanBergeijk, Klin, & Volkmar, 2008).

The majority of supports provided at institutions of higher education are carried out by traditional disability service personnel, who may not have expertise or extensive experience in supporting students with developmental disabilities such as autism spectrum disorder (Ellison, 2013; Hamblet, 2017). Most campus-based support services focus solely on academics and research has suggested that a lack of holistic on-campus services (e.g., housing assistance, social networking) is a barrier to PSE for students with disabilities (Dillon, 2007; Ellison et al., 2013; Hughes, 2009; Smith, 2007). The support of college students with disabilities is people-intensive, as carrying out effective services requires manpower and most institutions lack sufficient, appropriately trained personnel necessary to provide effective supports to students with disabilities (Ellison et al., 2013)

Disability-Related Barriers

Disability-related barriers specifically associated with developmental disabilities can affect a student's college experience and when combined with possible comorbid conditions, this may create significant challenges to success. Research exploring the experience of first-year college students with autism spectrum disorder found that those living with comorbid psychiatric disorders (e.g., high levels of anxiety) make poorer adjustments to college (Emmons, McCurry, Ellison, Klinger, & Klinger, 2010). Some college students with disabilities experience significant difficulties in areas important to building social networks, interpreting communication, connecting emotionally, and learning from others (Stansberry Brusnahan et al., 2017). Cognitive difficulties and executive functioning challenges can affect students' organizational skills and their completion of academic expectations. Challenges with emotional regulation, problem solving, and integrating sensory input can create barriers to an effective classroom experience (Gibbons & Goins, 2008). Students with disabilities can face challenges with the adaptive behaviors and academics (e.g., reading, writing, comprehension) expected of a college student (Berg, Jirikowic, Haerling, & MacDonald, 2017). Research has found that many students with disabilities lack an understanding of their challenges because of long-term concealment of their needs (Monteleone & Forrester-Jones, 2017). Additional challenges include navigating and managing systems such as transportation and financial management (Berg et al., 2017).

Effective Practices for High Schools

Research suggests that secondary education programs are failing to offer comprehensive transition programming to help students succeed in PSE (Nietupski, McQuillen, Berg, Daugherty, & Hamre-Niuetupski, 2001). Planning for transition supports from high school to PSE requires that the individualized education program (IEP) team considers the unique needs of the student. The following practices address some of the barriers students might encounter and focus on some of the skills needed to increase the probability for postsecondary success (Connor, 2012; Griffin, Lounds Taylor, Urbano, & Hodapp, 2014; Griffin & Papay, 2017, Hamblet, 2014; Szidon, Ruppar, & Smith, 2015).

CASE STUDY 7.1 (Collin)

After reviewing the benefits, Collin, a student with autism spectrum disorder and intellectual disability, felt a postsecondary education was the right next step for him after exiting high school. Just thinking about moving from high school into an unfamiliar environment that requires greater independence, autonomy, and self-determination skills was anxiety provoking for him. Collin's team and his family knew there would be barriers to higher education success, both institutional and directly related to disability characteristics, he would have to overcome. For example, Collin was not able to gain traditional admission so he was looking at a nontraditional inclusive college program for students with disabilities. With a postsecondary goal, his IEP team ensured they would prepare him with the skills he would need in the PSE settings. For example, they practiced self-disclosure of his disability, taught him how and when to access supports from a disability service office, took a field trip to a local college, provided opportunities for him to take an active role in making important decisions, and worked on other skills he needed for success in the postsecondary setting. Collin made a successful transition to a non-traditional college program where he acquired social skills, made friends, gained independence, acquired self-confidence, and learned critical job skills.

Provide Resources on Postsecondary Education

Because family members of transition-age youth with disabilities have cited the need for information on PSE (Griffin, McMillan, & Hodapp, 2010), educators should become familiar with relevant resources to support students with disabilities to attend college (Griffin & Papay, 2017). There are online resources for student with disabilities that provide information about how college is different from high school across various domains, including expectations and accommodations (e.g., Going to College, http://www.going-to-college.org; National Center for College Students With Disabilities, http://www.nccsdonline.org/; Think College, https://thinkcollege.net). Another way educators can provide information is to invite local college representatives and students with disabilities who are attending college to present at a high school class or event (Griffin & Papay, 2017; Hamblet, 2014).

Write Postsecondary Transition Goals Focused on Education

Utilizing person-centered planning, as outlined in Chapter 4, can help identify if a student is interested in PSE. When designing a transition IEP for a student interested in PSE, the team should examine possible college environments for the student and assess the skills necessary for success in those environments (Szidon et al., 2015). The IEP team should help the student identify preferences, interests, strengths, and needs in relation to these skills, and support students to set and meet goals that will contribute to success in college (Griffin & Papay, 2017). Using the data from transition assessments such as those discussed in Chapter 2, the IEP team should create a postsecondary goal (to be achieved after graduation) focused on education that has a clear connection to an aligned IEP goal (achieved annually during academic year; Szidon et al., 2015).

Plan for Active Student Involvement

Research has demonstrated that students who set PSE goals and actively participate in transition planning are more likely to achieve their goals than those who do not do so (Wei, Wagner, Hudson, Yu, & Javitz, 2016). The National Longitudinal Transition Study–2 (NLTS2) report revealed that even when students are present in IEP meetings, they do not actively participate (Cameto, Levine, & Wagner, 2004). Involvement in the transition-planning process is a way for students to develop and practice skills needed for success in college (Ankeny & Lehmann, 2011; Test et al., 2004). Educators can provide students with opportunities to engage in self-advocacy by supporting them in preparing a presentation for their IEP meeting about their present levels of performance, learning profile, and needed accommodations (Griffin & Papay, 2017; Hamblet, 2014; Lightner, Kipps-Vaughan, Schulte, & Trice, 2012). By fostering self-determination and helping students advocate for themselves in high school, educators provide practice so students can later engage in these skills in college (Griffin & Papay, 2017).

Take a Field Trip to a College

Educators can arrange a field trip to a disability services office at a local college, where the teachers, parents, and students can learn procedures for applying for services and accommodations and how to navigate a college campus (Hamblet, 2014, 2017). The college disability services staff can discuss the type of accommodations that are typically provided and those that are not likely to be approved (Hamblet, 2014). Students who self-identify and advocate for accommodations early in their college career have a greater likelihood of success, including achieving higher GPAs (Janiga & Costenbader, 2002; Lightner et al., 2012).

Teach and Practice Needed Skills

Educators play a crucial role in helping students gain the skills that they need to be successful in college. Teaching and practicing self-determination, organization, navigation, safety, and independence skills in high school helps prepare students for college (Connor & Lagares, 2007).

Self-determination skills. Self-determination skills (see Chapter 3) include decision making, problem solving, goal setting, self-management, self-awareness, self-knowledge, and self-advocacy (Shogren, 2013). Students who are aware of, accept, and can describe their disability—including articulating their preferences, interests, needs, and strengths—have a greater likelihood of succeeding in college (Connor, 2012; Getzel & Thoma, 2008; Griffin & Papay, 2017; Hamblet, 2014; Janiga & Costenbader, 2002; Milsom & Hartley, 2005; Trammell, 2003). In college, students are expected to self-advocate, which means they need to ask for their own accommodations. College students with disabilities will not have IEPs in college but can share information from a well-written Summary of Performance (SOP) from high school with the campus disability services office (Madaus & Shaw, 2006). The SOP provides information about the student's academic and nonacademic skills and suggests accommodations (Madaus, Bigaj, Chafouleas, & Simonsen, 2006; see Chapter 4).

The disability services office generally helps students with disabilities prepare a document to notify faculty of approved accommodations. Federal regulations provide students the right to disclose or not disclose their disabilities in college (Beale, 2005; Connor, 2012). Typically, it is the student's responsibility to disclose and give the recommended accommodation document to an instructor (Connor, 2012; Hamblet, 2017). Because of the importance of self-advocacy to college success, educators should engage students in activities aimed at teaching essential knowledge and skills (e.g., Oklahoma's Zarrow Center ME! Lessons for Teaching Self Awareness and Self-Advocacy; see also Cantley, Little, & Martin, 2010). Educators and parents should provide students opportunities to practice decision-making skills throughout high school and across multiple settings (i.e., school, home, and community; Connor, 2012). Educators can present students with scenarios highlighting challenging situations pertaining to college life (e.g., ramifications of playing video games versus studying for an exam) and engage students in processing and problem solving these situations (Connor, 2012; Troiano, 2003).

Study and organization skills. Explicitly teaching study and organization skills (e.g., when to complete assignments, how to manage time) can provide students with a strong foundation for using these skills in college (Lagares & Connor, 2009). Students should receive direct instruction so they develop digital literacy and other techniques that they can utilize independently and across a variety of skills, including organizing and managing their academic work (Connor, 2012; Deshler et al., 2008/2009; McMahon, Cihak, Wright, & Bell, 2016). Students also need to gain skills in determining manageable academic loads and how to schedule classes in a way that best enables their success.

Navigation skills. Many students with disabilities may experience challenges in independent navigation as they move from more self-contained or highly supported settings to a college campus (Griffin & Papay, 2017). Educators need to teach students the skills needed for independent navigation in school and coordinate with families to promote the use of navigation skills at home (Griffin & Papay, 2017). Educators can utilize technology to teach high school students a variety of skills, either on campus or in the community (Kelley, Test, & Cooke, 2013). Teaching students to use technology while they are in high school may improve chances that they will use the various technology supports that may be available in college (Hamblet, 2014).

Safety skills. Social naiveté and other characteristics of developmental disabilities make this population more vulnerable than their typically developing peers (Snell et al., 2009). Therefore, learning safety skills is vital for the well-being of students on campus. Educators and parents should work to identify areas of challenges and teach safety skills such as crossing the street safely, calling for help when in danger, and responding appropriately when being approached by a stranger (Fisher, Burke, & Griffin, 2013; Mechling, 2008).

Independence skills. A goal of education for all individuals, including those with disabilities, is to develop independence (Hadley, 2007). Parents and educators need to ensure that students are progressing toward the level of independence needed for success in the face of college-level rigor, both academically and socially (Banerjee & Brinckerhoff, 2009). As a student progresses through high school, the IEP team should reduce the level of support at school and home especially for accommodations or modifications less likely to be available in college (Hamblet, 2014, 2017). Fading supports can give students a sense of how they might perform in college. It is crucial that students be taught compensatory techniques prior to fading help so that they will be able to function without the accommodations or modifications (Banerjee & Brinckerhoff, 2009).

This list of practices to help students with disabilities transition into college is far from exhaustive. Preparing for success at college requires a focused effort by all involved parties, including the student. With a transition plan, teams can work toward developing opportunities to foster skill development. Given the difference in opportunities that a PSE affords, it is important to support students with disabilities to reduce barriers, learn skills, and help them succeed in college (Conner, 2012; Hamblet, 2011). Preparing students with disabilities with compensatory strategies and independence skills is essential to ensuring their success in college and in life.

Effective Practices for Higher Education

This section highlights promising practices in higher education that offer students with disabilities an inclusive experience that fosters growth, and which are supported by positive outcome data. College students with disabilities are most effectively supported by planned, individualized services designed to meet global and individual needs (Stansberry Brushnahan et al., 2017). To guide service providers as they prepare supports, Ellison, Hovatter, and Nelson (2013) developed the Benchmarks of Effective Supports for College Students Diagnosed With Autism Spectrum Disorder; these benchmarks can be used with students with developmental and intellectual disabilities as well. Faculty and staff must understand how to prepare an effective environment and provide a continuum of supports for the academic, social, and independent living needs of students with disabilities (see Table 7.2). The support of social and independent living needs can be as important as—and, in some cases, more important than—the support of academic needs for some students with disabilities.

Provide Universal Supports

Universal design involves designing environments readily accessible by a wide range of individuals preparing in advance to meet the challenges of diversity (Rose, Harbour, Johnston, Daley & Abarbanell, 2006). Universal design for learning focuses on accessible learning opportunities as influenced by three principles: information representation, knowledge expression, and learning engagement (see Table 7.3).

Provide Academic Supports

Effective postsecondary experiences offer learning opportunities in natural settings using naturally occurring supports (e.g., traditional disability support systems), augmenting those natural supports only when necessary (Grigal & Hart, 2010). To meet individual needs, person-centered planning (PCP; see Chapter 4) has been a standard practice in TPSID programs. PCP helps develop a course of study that ensures a student's preferences, interests, needs, and strengths are taken into account, which in turn motivates students to achieve individual goals (Grigal et al., 2015). Academic supports include traditional supports along with the use of digital technology, peer supports, and adaptive coaches.

Traditional academic support. Natural supports include access to traditional disability support and inclusive academic courses. Alignment with typical processes allows students with disabilities to participate more fully in campus

Table 7.2. Continuum of Supports

Tiers of support	Characteristics
Universal Support Promote a positive climate, provide financial resources, and ensure expertise to proactively and universally support students with disabilities on campus	• Culture: A well-informed campus with a culture to accept all students including those with disabilities • Finances: Dedicated finances to provide on-campus resources for students with disabilities • Expertise: On-campus expertise regarding disabilities with professionals available to educate, assist, and coach faculty and staff in effective pedagogy including universal design for learning
Academic Support Provide needed resources to support students' academic success on the college campus	• Resources: Staff to support students in their ability to identify and utilize crucial on- and off-campus resources • Academic support: Access to basic academic accommodations and reasonable modifications to support academic success for students with disabilities • Executive functioning support: Mentoring services that support students' organization needs (e.g., goal setting and meeting deadlines) and improve their ability to self-advocate • Mental health support: Mental health professionals trained in the unique needs of students with disabilities
Other Supports Provide supports to facilitate socialization and individual independence	Social support: Professionals and mentors who can assist students with the development of their on-campus social networks Independence: Staff available to facilitate social and independent skill building

Table 7.3. Universal Design for Learning (UDL) Principles

Principle	Description
Multiple means of representation	A focus area of UDL is teaching methods and techniques. When teaching, faculty should proactively plan multiple ways of presenting instruction and conveyance of knowledge recognizing students learn in diverse ways (Rose, Harbour, Johnston, Daley, & Abarbanell, 2006).
Multiple means of expression	A focus area of UDL is student expression of knowledge. When assessing learning, faculty should proactively plan multiple means for students to express learning recognizing there is not one optimal means for students to demonstrate acquisition of knowledge (Rose et al., 2006).
Multiple means of engagement	A focus area of UDL is student engagement in learning. When engaging students, faculty should proactively provide multiple methods to engage students in learning recognizing not all students are motivated by the same extrinsic rewards or conditions (Rose et al., 2006).

life, an important factor when the aim is to provide an authentic and inclusive college experience. Some students with disabilities are able to access higher education through traditional disability support services for academics and engage successfully with typical course offerings. Examples of traditional disability services within higher education includes extended testing time and note-taking assistance.

In a survey of programs available to students with ID, Grigal and colleagues (2012) found that half of the programs provided access to courses via the typical registration process and that students received academic advising in the same manner as other students. This demonstrates an alignment of the services of PSE programs with existing structures and processes used in college by all students, which is one of the standards of practice in the Think College Standards for Inclusive Higher Education (Grigal et al., 2012). When students with disabilities attend academically inclusive courses or classes that are a part of the typical college course catalog and available to all students in the college, they experience authentic experiences and accomplish real work, as opposed to an artificial curriculum designed for a separate classroom experience (Grigal & Hart, 2010). Students with disabilities can strategically select courses that suit their learning needs (e.g., hands-on experiences in highly engaging learning environments) and may actually do better within the model of higher education because they have the flexibility to take fewer courses at one time and their attention and focus does not need to be divided between multiple topics.

Individuals with disabilities experience characteristics to varying degrees and the unique needs of some students may extend beyond the scope of traditional disability services (Dillon, 2007; Ellison, Clark et al., 2013; Hughes, 2009). Faculty should be thoughtful of their instructional style as a means to accommodate the needs of students with disabilities. Suggestions for educators include:

- providing detailed instructions;
- providing clear deadlines for assignments;
- offering students a summary of key lecture points at the start and conclusion of class;
- using visual forms of information (e.g., PowerPoints);
- breaking down assignments into smaller, manageable chunks; and
- using peers to clarify assignments and answer basic questions for students with disabilities (Hughes, 2009).

Technology. Technology may provide effective academic supports for students with disabilities. Assistive technology increases access and support by limiting or overcoming barriers in the environment for individuals with disabilities. Assistive technology can range from "low-tech" (e.g., highlighters) to "high-tech" (e.g., computer technology). In the PSE environment, such technology can help students with disabilities compensate for organizational challenges caused by executive dysfunction, for example, by using simple tools such as online calendars and technology with alarms (Dillon, 2007). Laptop computers and other electronic devices may help students overcome motor challenges that otherwise might impede their note- and test-taking skills (Hughes, 2009).

Peer mentors. An advantage of accessing existing courses is that students with disabilities sit alongside their peers without disabilities, who can provide natural cues and demonstrate socially appropriate behaviors in the classroom. These experiences are indirect teachable moments that allow students with disabilities to initiate a task and develop their own reasoning skills without being prompted. Peer mentors are a way to provide both academic and social support to individuals with disabilities. For many students with disabilities, negotiating the social environment of a college campus may be the most challenging aspect of their college experience. Staff should ensure that designated peers receive training before working in a mentoring capacity (Hart et al., 2010). A majority of inclusive college programs use peers to provide supports to students, with these peer mentors viewed as an extension of program staff (Grigal et al., 2015).

Academic coaches. An academic coach works with a student using the student's preferences, interests, needs, and strengths to provide individualized support. This coach may accompany the student to class to provide cues about expected behaviors, as well as help interpret instructions and materials in a way that the student can understand. Coaching is viewed as a viable approach for students who need additional supports to be successful in college (Hart et al., 2010). An academic coach might be provided by a college program, or a service the student or family contracts. Faculty are becoming more acquainted with the use of the educational coaching model and adjusting to having another person sitting in their classroom. Just as with peer mentors, adaptive coaches need to receive training so that they understand their role in the classroom and how best to assist individuals with disabilities in study times outside of class. In addition, students with disabilities also need training on the role of the coach. They need to understand their own responsibilities in meeting deadlines, ensure that their work is authentic, and be responsive to the input of the coach. Students with disabilities should take a collaborative role in developing strategies guided by the coach (Butler, Elaschuk, & Poole, 2000).

Accommodations. An important component to academic access for students with disabilities is receiving necessary accommodations. The most common accommodations are academic supports, such as note takers and readers. Students also receive enrollment accommodations, such as modified course loads, substitutes for required courses, and priority registration. Academic accommodations can also be granted, such as access to instructors' notes, advance access to materials, extended time and alternate settings for exams, and alternative test formats (Grigal et al., 2015).

Social networks. Facilitating the development of social networks is key to providing a well-rounded college experience for students with disabilities. A literature review by Test and colleagues (2009) showed a strong association between greater social competence, increased PSE participation, and improved employment outcomes after leaving high school. Based on student interviews, Folk, Yamamoto, and Stodden (2012) reported that opportunity for social interaction presented by participation in PSE was a prevalent theme, and students who live in campus housing generally have higher levels of participation in social activities

(Grigal et al., 2015). In Grigal and colleagues' study (2015), 95% of students living on campus reported going out with personal friends, compared to 49% living with family and 76% living in off-campus, non-family housing (Grigal et al., 2015).

The closer in proximity students with disabilities are to college students without disabilities, the more opportunities there are for spontaneous participation in the social life on campus. These spontaneous interactions range from going to athletic events to gathering on the residence hall floor to watch a movie in the lounge, or meeting up with a friend for a late-night beverage in the student commons. Students with disabilities that reside off campus have less spontaneous participation in social activities. This may be attributed to the fact that commuter students have to make plans ahead of time to get onto campus for activities, and transportation may involve a higher level of coordination and additional cost. In addition, transportation options may not always be available if spontaneous opportunities for participation on campus occurs later in the evening.

Provide Other Needed Supports

Traditional disability services, due to a lack of resources and expertise, may be lacking in the ability to support the social needs of students with disabilities (Ellison, Clark et al., 2013). Services designed to support social needs are essential to success for students with disabilities in higher education settings. In fact, social supports may be even more critical for postsecondary success than academic supports (Ellison, Clark et al., 2013). Some areas in which support may be necessary include campus housing, social skills, independent living, and mental health.

Campus housing. Navigating the community that is a college or university campus may be daunting to students with disabilities (Dillon, 2007; Ellison, Clark et al., 2013; Hughes, 2009). The social networking inherent within campus housing may pose significant challenges for students with disabilities (Hughes, 2009). Students' challenges related to social skills and social communication may prevent them from fully advocating for their on-campus needs, including making appropriate and timely decisions regarding self-disclosure (Ellison, Clark et al., 2013). A well-informed community appears important to supporting students with disabilities.

Social support. Anticipating the social needs of students with disabilities affords disability services professionals the opportunity to develop basic systemic supports that may reduce social anxiety, such as providing students with an early and detailed schedule of orientation and identifying quiet, less-populated cafeteria spaces in which students may eat meals (Hughes, 2009). Research has highlighted the importance of assessing social skill challenges, and of formalizing individual and group activities that promote the development of skills to meet identified needs (Dillon, 2007; Ellison, Hovatter et al., 2013).

Independent living. College students with disabilities are often challenged by having underdeveloped adaptive and independent living skills (Ellison, Clark et al., 2013). Students within this population tend to struggle with transition, flexibility, free time, and self-advocacy (Wolf, Brown, & Bork Kuikiela, 2009). A college campus is a complex society with hidden curriculum, rules, protocols, and customs that can overwhelm a student with a disability (VanBergeijk et al., 2008). Regularly scheduled meetings with a mentor or coach may be beneficial to students to improve social and independent living skills and provide additional or explicit opportunities for social networking.

Mental health services. Access to appropriate on-campus mental health services appears important to the success of PSE students with mental health needs (VanBergeijk et al., 2008). Due to challenges related to their disability, students who need mental health services may not recognize the need or attempt to access mental health services, highlighting the need for a campus community well-informed about disability (Ellison, Clark et al., 2013). Students with disabilities may need to rely on faculty, staff, and peers to provide unsolicited advice about seeking mental health services. There is concern that on-campus mental health services may be generally ineffective in meeting the needs of this student population (Ellison, Clark et al., 2013).

Summary

In response to the growing numbers of students with developmental disabilities, including those with autism spectrum disorder and ID, who wish to continue their education beyond high school, institutes of higher education across the country have begun to provide opportunities (Neubert, Moon, Grigal, & Redd, 2001). In this chapter, we have described the benefits of participation in higher education for students with disabilities. We presented two higher education models to facilitate the inclusion of students with disabilities. We addressed challenges both institutional and directly related to disability characteristics. Most important, we highlighted effective practices in high school and at the PSE level to meet the needs of students with disabilities.

References

ADA Amendments Act of 2008, Pub. L. No. 110-325, 122 Stat. 3553, to be codified at 42 U.S.C. § 12101 (2009).

Alper, S. (2003). The relationship between inclusion and other trends in education. In D. Ryndak & S. Alper (Eds.), *Curriculum and instruction for students with significant disabilities in inclusive setting* (2nd ed., pp. 13-30). Boston, MA: Allyn & Bacon.

Alwell, M., & Cobb, B. (2009). Functional life skills curricular interventions for youth with disabilities: A systematic review. *Career Development for Exceptional Individuals, 32*, 82–93. 10.1177/0885728809336656

Ankeny, E. M., & Lehmann, J. P. (2011). Journey toward self-determination: Voices of students with disabilities who participated in a secondary transition program on a community college campus. *Remedial and Special Education, 32*, 279–289. doi:10.1177/0741932510362215

Banerjee, M., & Brinckerhoff, L. C. (2009). Helping students with disabilities navigate the college admissions process. In S. F. Shaw, J. W. Madaus, & L. L. Dukes (Eds.), *Preparing students with disabilities for college success: A practical guide to transition planning* (pp. 229–256). Baltimore, MD: Brookes.

Baum, S., Ma, J., & Payea, K. (2013). *Education pays 2013: The benefits of higher education for individuals and society*. Washington, DC: The College Board. Retrieved from https://trends.collegeboard.org/sites/default/files/education-pays-2013-full-report.pdf

Beale, A. (2005). Preparing students with learning disabilities for postsecondary education: Their rights and responsibilities. *Techniques: Connecting Education and Careers, 80*(3), 24–27.

Berg, L. A., Jirikowic, T., Haerling, K., & MacDonald, G. (2017). Navigating the hidden curriculum of higher education for postsecondary students with intellectual disabilities. *American Journal of Occupational Therapy, 71*(3), 1–8. doi:10.5014/ajot.2017.024703

Bouck, E. C. (2010). Reports of life skill training for students with intellectual disabilities in and out of school. *Journal of Intellectual Disability Research, 54*, 1093–1103. doi:10.1111/j.1365-2788.2010.01339.x

Butler, D. L., Elaschuk, C. L., & Poole, S. (2000). Promoting strategic writing by postsecondary students with learning disabilities: A report of three case studies. *Learning Disability Quarterly, 23*, 196–213. http://dx.doi.org/10.2307/1511164

Cameto, R., Levine, P., & Wagner, M. (2004). *Transition planning for students with disabilities. A special topic report from the National Longitudinal Transition Study–2 (NLTS2)*. Menlo Park, CA: SRI International.

Cantley, P., Little, K., & Martin, J. (2010). *Me! Lessons for teaching selfawareness & self-advocacy*. Norman, OK: Zarrow Center for Learning Enrichment. Retrieved from http://ou.edu/education/centers-and-partnerships/zarrow/transition-education-materials/me-lessons-for-teaching-self-awareness-and-self-advocacy

Carnevale, A. P., Rose, S. J., & Cheah, B. (2011). *The college payoff: Education, occupations, lifetime earnings*. Washington, DC: Georgetown University Center on Education and the Workforce. Retrieved from https://cew.georgetown.edu/cew-reports/the-college-payoff/#full-report

Cobb, B., Lehmann, J., Newman-Gonchar, R., & Alwell, M. (2009). Self-determination for students with disabilities: A narrative metasynthesis. *Career Development and Transition for Exceptional Individuals, 32*, 108–114. doi:10.1177/0885728809336654

Connor, D. J. (2012). Helping students with disabilities transition to college: 21 tips for students with LD and/or ADD/ADHD. *TEACHING Exceptional Children, 44*(5), 16–25. doi:10.1177/004005991204400502

Connor, D. J., & Lagares, C. (2007). Facing high stakes in high school: 25 successful strategies from an inclusive social studies classroom. *TEACHING Exceptional Children, 40*(2), 18–27. doi:10.1177/004005990704000203

de Araujo, P., & Murray, J. M. (2010). Channels for improved performance—From living on campus. *American Journal of Business Education, 3*(12), 57–64.

Deshler, D. D., Schumaker, J. B., Lenz, B. K., Bulgren, J. A., Hock, M. F., Knight, J., & Ehren, B. J. (2008/2009). Ensuring content-area learning by secondary students with LD. *Journal of Education, 129*, 169–181.

Dillon, M. R. (2007). Creating supports for college students with Asperger syndrome through collaboration. *College Student Journal, 41*, 499–504.

Ellison, L. M. (2013). *Assessing the readiness of higher education to instruct and support students with Asperger's disorder* (Doctoral dissertation). Marshall University, Huntington, WV. Retrieved from http://mds.marshall.edu/cgi/viewcontent.cgi?article=1428&context=etd

Ellison, M., Clark, J., Cunningham, M., & Hansen, R. (2013). Academic and campus accommodations that foster success for college students with Asperger's disorder. In F. Kochan, L. Searby, & M. Barakat (Eds.), *Southern Regional Council on Educational Administration 2013 Yearbook: Jazzing It Up* (pp. 65–76). Alabama: Auburn University College of Education. Retrieved from http://srcea.msstate.edu/yearbook/2013Yearbook.pdf

Ellison, M., Hovatter, P., & Nelson, A. (2013, July 12). *Developing a therapeutic relationship with clients diagnosed with Asperger's disorder*. Session at the 44th Autism Society National Conference and Exposition, Pittsburgh, PA.

Emmons, J., McCurry, S., Ellison, M., Klinger, M. R., & Klinger, L. G. (2010, May 21). *College programs for students with ASD: Predictors of successful college transition*. Poster session, 9th Annual International Meeting for Autism Research (IMFAR), Philadelphia, PA.

Farrell, E. F. (2004). Asperger's confounds colleges. *Chronicle of Higher Education, 51*(7), 35–36. Retrieved from https://www.chronicle.com/article/Aspergers-Confounds-Colleges/25314

Fisher, M. H., Burke, M. M., & Griffin, M. M. (2013). Teaching young adults with intellectual and developmental disabilities to respond appropriately to lures from strangers. *Journal of Applied Behavior Analysis, 46*, 528–533. doi:10.1002/jaba.32

Folk, E. D. R., Yamamoto, K. K., & Stodden, R. A. (2012). Implementing inclusion and collaborative teaming in a model program of postsecondary education for young adults with intellectual disabilities. *Journal of Policy and Practice in Intellectual Disabilities, 9*, 257–269. doi:10.1111/jppi.12007

Getzel, E. E., & Thoma, C. A. (2008). Experiences of college students with disabilities and the importance of self-determination in higher education settings. *Career Development for Exceptional Individuals, 31*, 77–84. doi:10.1177/0885728808317658

Gibbons, M. M., & Goins, S. (2008). Getting to know the child with Asperger syndrome. *Professional School Counseling, 11*, 347–352. doi:10.5330/PSC.n.2010-11.347

Gilmore, S., Bose, J., & Hart, D. (2001). Postsecondary education as a critical step toward meaningful employment: Vocational rehabilitation's role. *Research to Practice, 7*(4), 1–4.

Griffin, M. M., Lounds Taylor, J., Urbano, R. C., & Hodapp, R. M. (2014). Involvement in transition planning meetings among high school students with autism spectrum disorders. *The Journal of Special Education, 47*(4) 256–264. doi:10.1177/0022466913475668

Griffin, M. M., McMillan, E. D., & Hodapp, R. M. (2010). Family perspectives on postsecondary education for students with intellectual disabilities. *Education and Training in Autism and Developmental Disabilities, 45*, 339–346.

Griffin, M. M., & Papay, C. K. (2017). Supporting students with intellectual and developmental disabilities to attend college. *TEACHING Exceptional Children, 49*, 411–419. doi: 10.1177/0040059917711695

Grigal, M., & Hart, D. (2010). *Think college! Postsecondary education options for students with intellectual disabilities*. Baltimore, MD: Paul H. Brookes.

Grigal, M., Hart, D., Smith, F. A., Domin, D., Sulewski, J., & Weir, C. (2015). *Think College National Coordinating Center. Annual report on the transition and postsecondary programs for students with intellectual disabilities year 4 (2013–2014)*. Boston, MA: University of Massachusetts Boston, Institute for Community Inclusion. Retrieved from https://thinkcollege.net/sites/default/files/files/resources/year4_Final.pdf

Grigal, M., Hart, D., Smith, F. A., Domin, D., & Weir, C. (2017). *Think College National Coordinating Center. Annual report on the transition and postsecondary programs for students with intellectual disabilities year 5 (2014–2015)*. Boston, MA: University of Massachusetts Boston, Institute for Community Inclusion. Retrieved from http://programs.thinkcollege.net/sites/default/files/files/resources/year5_web_F.pdf

Grigal, M., Hart, D., & Weir, C. (2012). A survey of postsecondary education programs for students with intellectual disabilities in the United States. *Journal of Policy and Practice in Intellectual Disabilities, 9*, 223–233. doi:10.1111/jppi.12012

Grigal, M., Neubert, D. A., & Moon, S. M. (2002). Postsecondary options for students with significant disabilities. *TEACHING Exceptional Children, 35*(2), 68–73. doi:10.1177/004005990203500210

Grigal, M., Weir, C., Hart, D., & Opsal, C., (2013). The impact of college on self-determination. *National Gateway to Self-Determination Issue 6: Self-Determination and Postsecondary Education*, 1–3. Retrieved from http://ngsd.org/sites/default/files/research_to_practice_sd_-_issue_6.pdf

Hadley, W. M. (2007). The necessity of academic accommodations for first-year college students with learning disabilities. *Journal of College Admission, 195*, 9–13.

Hafner, D. (2008). *Inclusion in postsecondary education: Phenomenological study on identifying and addressing barriers to inclusion of individuals with significant disabilities as a four-year liberal arts college* (Doctoral dissertation). Edgewood College, Madison, WI.

Hafner, D., & Moffatt, C. (2012). *Cutting-Edge report 2007–2012*. Madison, WI: Edgewood College.

Hamblet, E. C. (2011). *7 steps for success: High school to college transition strategies for students with disabilities*. Arlington, VA: Council for Exceptional Children.

Hamblet, E. C. (2014). Nine strategies to improve college transition planning for students with disabilities. *TEACHING Exceptional Children, 46*(3), 53–59. doi:10.1177/004005991404600306

Hamblet, E. C. (2017). *From high school to college: Steps to success for students with disabilities* (2nd ed.). Arlington, VA: Council for Exceptional Children.

Hart, D., Grigal, M., & Weir, C. (2010). Expanding the paradigm: Postsecondary education options for individuals with autism spectrum disorder and intellectual disabilities. *Focus on Autism and Other Developmental Disabilities, 25*, 134–150. doi:10.1177/1088357610373759

Hart, D., Zimbrich, K., & Parker, D. (2005). Dual enrollment as a postsecondary education option for students with intellectual disabilities. In E. Getzel & P. Wehman (Eds.), *Going to college: Expanding opportunities for people with disabilities* (pp. 253–266). Baltimore, MD: Paul H. Brookes.

Hartz, E. J. (2014). *Outcomes of inclusive postsecondary education for students with intellectual disabilities at Edgewood College* (Doctoral dissertation). Edgewood College, Madison, WI.

Hughes, J. (2009). Higher education and Asperger's syndrome. *Chronicle of Higher Education, 55*(40), 21.

Individuals With Disabilities Education Act, 20 U.S.C. §§ 1400 *et seq*. (2006 & Supp. V. 2011).

Janiga, S. J., & Costenbader, V. (2002). The transition from high school to postsecondary education for students with learning disabilities: A survey of college service coordinators. *Journal of Learning Disabilities, 35*, 462–468, 479. doi:10.1177/00222194020350050601

Kelley, K. R., Test, D. W., & Cooke, N. L. (2013). Effects of picture prompts delivered by a video iPod on pedestrian navigation. *Exceptional Children, 79*, 459–474. doi:10.1177/001440291307900405

Lagares, C., & Connor, D. J. (2009). 20 ways to help students prepare for high school examinations. *Intervention in School and Clinic, 45*, 63–67. doi:10.1177/1053451209338399

Lightner, K. L., Kipps-Vaughan, D., Schulte, T., & Trice, A. D. (2012). Reasons university students with a learning disability wait to seek disability services. *Journal of Postsecondary Education and Disability, 25*, 159–177.

Lindstrom, L., Doren, B., & Miesch, J. (2011). Waging a living: Career development and long-term employment outcomes for young adults with disabilities. *Exceptional Children, 77*, 423–434. doi:10.1177/001440291107700403

Madaus, J. W. (2011). The history of disability services in higher education. *New Directions for Higher Education, 154*, 5–15. doi:10.1002/he.429

Madaus, J. W., Bigaj, S., Chafouleas, S. M., & Simonsen, B. M. (2006). What key information can be included in a comprehensive summary of performance? *Career Development for Exceptional Individuals, 29*, 90–99. doi:10.1177/08857288060290020701

Madaus, J. W., & Shaw, S. F. (2004). Section 504: The differences in the regulations regarding secondary and postsecondary education. *Intervention in School and Clinic, 40*, 81–87. doi:10.1177/10534512040400020301

Madaus, J. W., & Shaw, S. F. (2006). The impact of the IDEA 2004 on transition to college for students with learning disabilities. *Learning Disabilities Research & Practice, 21*, 273–281. doi:10.1111/j.1540-5826.2006.00223.x

McGregor, K. K., Langenfeld, N., Van Horne, S., Oleson, J., Anson, M., & Jacobson, W. (2016). The university experiences of students with learning disabilities. *Learning Disabilities Research and Practice, 31*, 90–102. doi:10.1111/ldrp.12102

McMahon, D., Cihak, D. F., Wright, R. E., & Bell, S. M. (2016). Augmented reality for teaching science vocabulary to postsecondary education students with intellectual disabilities and autism. *Journal of Research on Technology in Education, 48*, 38–56. doi:10.1080/15391523.2015.1 103149

Mechling, L. (2008). Thirty-year review of safety skill instruction for persons with intellectual disabilities. *Education and Training in Autism & Developmental Disabilities, 43*, 311–323.

Milsom, A., & Hartley, M. T. (2005). Assisting college students with learning disabilities transitioning to college: What school counselors should know. *Professional School Counseling 8*, 436–441.

Monteleone, R., & Forrester-Jones, R. (2017). "Disability means, um, dysfunctioning people." A qualitative analysis of the meaning and experience of disability among adults with intellectual disabilities. *Journal of Applied Research in Intellectual Disabilities, 30*, 301–315. doi:10.1111/jar.12240

Moon, M. S., Grigal, M., & Neubert, D. (2001). High school and beyond. *The Exceptional Parent, 31*(7), 52–57.

Neubert, D. A., Moon, M. S., Grigal, M., & Redd, V. (2001). Postsecondary educational practices for individuals with mental retardation and other significant disabilities: A review of the literature. *Journal of Vocational Rehabilitation, 16*, 155–168.

Neubert, D. A., Moon, M. S., Grigal, M., & Redd, V. (2002). Postsecondary education and transition services for students ages 18–21 with significant disabilities. *Focus on Exceptional Children, 34*(8), 1–11.

Nietupski, J., McQuillen, D., Berg, D., Daughtery, V., & Hamre-Nietupski, S. (2001). Preparing students with mild disabilities for careers in technology: A process and recommendations from Iowa's High School High Tech program. *Journal of Vocational Rehabilitation, 16*, 179–188.

Rehabilitation Act of 1973, as amended by Pub. L. No. 110-325, to be codified at 29 U.S.C. § 701 (2009).

Rose, D. H., Harbour, W. S., Johnston, C. S., Daley, S. G., & Abarbanell, L. (2006). Universal design for learning in postsecondary education: Reflections on principles and their application. *Journal of Postsecondary Education and Disability, 19*, 135–151.

Shogren, K. A. (2013). *Self-determination and transition planning*. Baltimore, MD: Paul H. Brookes.

Smith, C. P. (2007). Support services for students with Asperger's syndrome in higher education. *College Student Journal, 41*, 515–531.

Snell, M. E., Luckasson, R., Borthwick-Duffy, W. S., Bradley, V., Buntinx, W. H., Coulter, D. L., … Schalock, R. L. (2009). Characteristics and needs of people with intellectual disability who have higher IQs. *Intellectual and Developmental Disabilities, 47*, 220–233. doi:10.1352/1934-9556-47.3.220

Stansberry Brushnahan, L. L., Ellison, M., & Hafner, D. (2017). The transition from high school to higher education: Inclusive services and supports. In D. Zager, D. Chiak, & A. Stone-MacDonald (Eds.), *Autism spectrum disorders: Identification, education, and treatment* (4th ed., pp. 340–375). New York, NY: Routledge.

Szidon, K., Ruppar, A., & Smith, L. (2015). Five steps for developing effective transition plans for high school students with autism spectrum disorder. *TEACHING Exceptional Children, 47*, 147–152. doi:10.1177/0040059914559780

Test, D. W., Mason, C., Hughes, C., Konrad, M., Neale, M., & Wood, W. M. (2004). Student involvement in individualized education program meetings. *Exceptional Children, 70*, 391–412. doi:10.1177/001440290407000401

Test, D. W., Mazzotti, V. L. Mustian, A. L., Fowler, C. H., Kortering, L., & Kohler, P. (2009). Evidenced-based predictors for improving postschool outcomes for students with disabilities. *Career Development for Exceptional Individuals, 32*, 160–181. doi:10.1177/0885728809346960

Trammell, J. K. (2003). The impact of academic accommodations on final grades in a postsecondary setting. *Journal of College Reading and Learning, 34*, 76–89. doi:10.1080/10790195.2003.10850157

Troiano, P. F. (2003). College students and learning disability: Elements of self-style. *Journal of College Student Development, 44*, 404–419. doi:10.1353/csd.2003.0033

Uditsky, B., & Hughson, E. (2012). Inclusive postsecondary education—An evidence-based moral imperative. *Journal of Policy and Practice in Intellectual Disabilities, 9*, 298–302. doi:10.1111/jppi.12005

VanBergeijk, E., Klin, A., & Volkmar, F. (2008). Supporting more able students on the autism spectrum: College and beyond. *Journal of Autism and Developmental Disorders, 38*, 1359–1370. doi:10.1007/s10803-007-0524-8

Wehmeyer, M. L., Abery, B. H., Zhang, D., Ward, K., Willis, D., Hossain, W. A., & Walker, H. M. (2011). Personal self-determination and moderating variables that impact efforts to promote self-determination. *Exceptionality, 19*, 19–30. doi:10.1080/09362835.2011.537225

Wei, X., Wagner, M., Hudson, L., Yu, J. W., & Javitz, H. (2016). The effect of transition planning participation and goal-setting on college enrollment among youth with autism spectrum disorders. *Remedial and Special Education, 37*, 3–14. doi:10.1177/0741932515581495

Wolf, L., Brown, J., & Bork Kuikiela, R. (2009). *Students with Asperger syndrome: A guide for college personnel*. Shawnee Mission, KS: AAPC.

Zager, D., & Smith, T. (2012). *Inclusion at the postsecondary level for students with autism spectrum disorders* (Division on Autism and Developmental Disabilities Position Paper). Retrieved from http://daddcec.org/Portals/0/CEC/Autism_Disabilities/Research/Position_Papers/Inclusion%20at%20the%20Postsecondary%20Level%20for%20Students%20with%20Autism%20Spectrum%20Disorders%20.pdf

CHAPTER 8
Community Participation and Supports
Emily C. Bouck and Erik W. Carter

Objectives:
- Define community-based instruction and how to teach real-world skills (e.g., community participation; personal health and safety; home living; travel and mobility; socialization, recreation, and leisure).
- Discuss how to increase the capacity and commitment of communities to meaningfully include students with disabilities, as well as interventions that engage partners (e.g., parents, community leaders, congregations) in community change efforts that enable students to live rich and personally satisfying lives after high school.

This chapter focuses on community-based instruction and strategies—such as real-life skills—to prepare youth and young adults with developmental disabilities, including those with autism spectrum disorder and intellectual disability, to live as independently as possible and function successfully in an inclusive society. Community-based instruction is an instructional format that bridges community participation with instructional preparation. In other words, this type of instruction involves students learning skills in natural settings. In this chapter, we discuss the real-life skills required for successful integration and functioning within natural environments.

Key Terminology	
Real-life skills	Authentic skills needed for real-life involvement, participation, and success in one's current and subsequent environments (Bouck, Taber-Doughty, & Savage, 2015).

Key Terminology (cont'd)	
Community-based instruction	An instructional format that bridges community participation with instructional preparation.
Community conversation	An asset-based approach for identifying and engaging a diverse group of local stakeholders in addressing the needs of transition-age youth and young adults with disabilities (Carter & Bumble, 2018; Carter, Owens, Swedeen, et al., 2009).
Community mapping	An approach that involves identifying and compiling the informal and formal resources and opportunities that might be drawn upon to connect students to community life and improve outcomes for youth with disabilities (Crane & Mooney, 2005; Tindle, Leconte, Buchanan, & Taymans, 2005).

Real-life skills are skills that support a student's successful independent living post-high school and encourage inclusive community participation (Bouck, Taber-Doughty, & Savage, 2015; Clark, Field, Patton, Brolin, & Sitlington, 1994; Storey & Miner, 2011; see Table 8.1). Hence, real-life skills focus broadly on all facets of inclusive communities: working, living, and having fun (i.e., leisure and recreation; Brown et al., 1979). Real-life skills can be likened to functional or daily living skills, but are more precisely focused on the skills each student needs for real-life involvement, participation, and success. Real-life skills are not superficial or artificial skills, but are authentic to one's current and subsequent environments (Bouck et al., 2015).

As implied, real-life skills represent an umbrella under which a variety of skills to promote independent living and community participation fall, including access to community, daily living skills, vocational education, postsecondary education skills, financial skills, social or relationship skills, transportation skills, self-determination skills, and functional academics. Many of these skills are covered in other chapters in this book (e.g., postsecondary education, employment), and will not be extensively discussed in this chapter; the reader is invited to review those chapters within this book for additional information.

Table 8.1. Real-Life Skills

Skill	Examples of focus
Functional academics	Literacy: Sight word recognition, reading for pleasure or leisure, writing or signing one's name Mathematics: Time management, number recognition (e.g., phone numbers), money skills
Vocational education	Career exploration; job shadowing
Financial	Keeping a budget, using bank services, cashing a check
Community access	Use of laundromats, grocery stores, restaurants
Independent living	Obtaining and maintaining a household
Daily living	Food preparation; housekeeping; personal maintenance or hygiene; safety skills
Transportation	Walking, riding a bus, driving a car, using ride services
Self-determination	Problem solving, making one's own decisions
Social/relationships	Developing friendships, appropriate interacting with others in various settings (e.g., work, home, community)
Leisure and recreation	Hobbies, recreation (e.g., bowling, movies)

Note. Adapted from *Footsteps Toward the Future: Implementing a Real-World Curriculum for Students With Disabilities*, by E. C. Bouck, T. Taber-Doughty, and M. N. Savage, 2015, p. 35. Copyright 2015 by the Council for Exceptional Children. See also Browder & Snell (1993); Cronin & Patton (1993); Dattilo & Hoge, 1999; Gajar, Goodmand, & McAfree (1993); Retish, Hitchings, Horvath, & Schmalle (1991); Sands & Doll (1996); Snell & Browder (1987); Storey & Miner, 2011; Wehmeyer, Sands, Knowlton, & Kozleski, 2002; Westling & Fox (2000).

Instruction in real-life skills dates back many decades to the 1930s (Kolstoe, 1970). At one point, a curriculum emphasizing real-life skills (i.e., a functional curriculum or life skills curriculum) was the predominant educational programming for students with intellectual disability and other developmental disabilities (Kolstoe, 1970). A decline in focus on real-life skills instruction in schools coincided with an increase in attention to more academic and standards-based instruction for this population of students (Bouck, 2012). However, the two approaches—real-life skills and skills—do not need to be polarized (Ayres, Lowrey, Douglas, & Sievers, 2011). Real-life skills and academic skills exist within a continuum, and both skills can be taught to students through such approaches as embedding real-life skills into academic instruction and embedding academic skills into real-life skills instruction (Bouck, 2012; Bouck et al., 2015; Collins, Karl, Riggs, Galloway, & Hager, 2010). The infusion of academic skills within a life-skills curriculum means that one's primary educational programing is focused on real-life skills; educators work to embed academic components within the life skills where there is a natural connection. For example, in teaching price comparison (a real-life skill), educators can take the opportunity to teach students about decimals. Conversely, when embedding real-life skills within an academically oriented educational programing, educators can focus on students learning to determine and select the lower priced item (among two or three choices) as an instructional activity relevant to the standard involving solving equations (Bouck, 2017b).

Regardless of one's position towards the perceived dichotomy of real-life skills versus academic skills, research supports giving attention to real-life skills for secondary students with disabilities. In a review of evidence-based practices focused on transition, Test and colleagues (2009) found life-skills instruction to have strong evidence supporting its focus in secondary education. In fact, they found many real-life skills—such as purchasing, financial, and daily living (cooking, shopping) skills; leisure and recreation; functional academics; and self-determination—to have moderate or strong levels of evidence supporting their use. Similarly, Mazzotti, Rowe, Cameto, Test, and Morningstar (2013) concluded that independent living skills (i.e., real-life skills) were positive predictors of postsecondary education, employment, and independent living for secondary students with disabilities.

Evidence-Based Practices and Strategies

Few evidence-based syntheses have addressed real-life skills collectively. However, there exist practices and strategies with evidence and research to support their use regarding real-life skills.

Systematic instruction is supported throughout the literature as an evidence-based practice for teaching daily living (i.e., real-life) skills to students with developmental disabilities (Browder, Wood, Thompson, & Ribuffo, 2014). Systematic instruction represents a wide variety of approaches associated with applied behavior analysis principles, such as means of prompting (e.g., system of least prompts and time delay) and providing reinforcement (Browder et al., 2014;

Spooner, Browder, & Mims, 2011). Table 8.2 provides examples of systematic instruction (see Shurr, Jimenez, & Bouck, in press, for a more in-depth discussion). Although different systemic instruction approaches can be used individually, often they are combined as part of a treatment or intervention package.

Table 8.2. Examples of Systematic Instruction

Strategy	Description and example
System of least prompts	Students are provided prompts in a sequential order that moves from the least intrusive to the most intrusive (e.g., full physical support).
	Example: In teaching students to compare grocery item prices, Bouck, Satsangi, & Bartlett (2016) used the system of least prompts to support secondary students with developmental disabilities to compare prices with numbers lines and audio recorders. The prompting hierarchy consisted of verbal question, verbal direction, gesture plus verbal direction, model and verbal direction, and hand-over-hand plus verbal direction.
Constant time delay	Students are given prompts or assistance after a constant (set) period of time if the student does not initiate the behavior or response.
	Example: Seward, Schuster, Ault, Collins, & Hall (2014) used constant time delay to teach the leisure skill of playing cards to secondary students with intellectual disability.
Task analysis	Students are taught a complex task or behavior (i.e., referred to as chained) by breaking that task into smaller components, typically each consisting of one step.
	Example: Bouck, Savage, Meyer, Taber-Doughty, & Hunley (2014) used a task analysis of recipes, along with self-monitoring and the system of least prompts, to assist student in acquiring independent cooking skills.

Technology-aided interventions represent another approach widely used to teach real-life skills to youth and young adults with disabilities. One of the most common technology approaches—and an evidence-based approach for students with autism spectrum disorder for real-life skills as well as other skill domains—is video modeling (Hong et al., 2016; Wong et al., 2015). *Video modeling* is when a student is shown a video of a task or skill and then completes said task after watching the whole video (Cannella-Malone et al., 2011). *Video prompting* is similar to video modeling, but a student watches each component step of a task on video and completes that step before moving on to the next step (Cannella-Malone et al., 2011). Commonly, video modeling or video prompting to support real-life skills is completed on mobile devices (e.g., smartphones or tablets; Ayres, Mechling, & Sansosti, 2013). In addition to video modeling or prompting, which rely on more sophisticated technology (e.g., mobile devices), low-tech options also support students with disabilities with prompting (Bouck, 2017a). Students with disabilities can receive their prompting via pictures (i.e., picture prompting) or by audio (i.e., audio prompting). *Audio prompting* can occur through a variety of devices (e.g., audio recorders, smart phones; Bouck et al., 2015). Often, video, audio, and picture prompts are delivered on devices in such a manner that, once created, the student can operate the tool independently to acquire, maintain, or generalize real-life skills. These promptings systems are often referred to as *self-operated prompting systems* (Mechling, Gast, & Seid, 2010; see Table 8.3 for steps on developing picture, audio, and video self-operated prompting systems).

Another evidence-based practice relative to real-life skills is **community-based instruction** (i.e., in vivo; Test et al., 2009). In other words, it is more beneficial to provide instruction in real-life skills in the real—or community-based—settings in which skills would naturally occur, rather than a simulated setting (i.e., an approximation of the real setting; Test, Spooner, Holzberg, Roberston, & Davis, 2016). For example, when teaching price comparison skills, researchers have suggested teaching students to compare prices in a grocery store rather than a simulated grocery store in a classroom (Test et al., 2009).

Identifying Community Opportunities and Supports

As noted, instruction addressing real-life skills can be enhanced when students with disabilities are taught those skills in community settings beyond the high school campus. Likewise, inclusion in community activities provides an authentic context for students to practice and refine these skills over time. Unfortunately, community participation can be quite limited for youth and young adults with disabilities (Amado, Stancliffe, McCarron, & McCallion, 2013; Carter et al., 2010). Secondary educators, in partnership with others within and beyond the school, can play an important role in expanding these essential opportunities.

There is a tendency among educators and families to think first (or even exclusively) about community opportunities and supports that are designed specifically for students with disabilities, such as specialized recreation programs (e.g., Special Olympics), friendship groups (e.g., Best Buddies), disability employment providers, "special needs" ministries, or community and day programs. But most communities offer a much wider array of opportunities and programs that can connect students to enjoyable activities and help them develop the skills and supports they need to participate fully in their community. Identifying and accessing these natural community supports is an important element of high-quality transition education (Hughes & Carter, 2011; Test, Smith, & Carter, 2014). Two particular approaches can be especially practical for transition teams: community mapping and community conversations.

Community Mapping

Community mapping involves identifying and compiling the informal and formal resources and opportunities that might be drawn upon to connect students to community life and improve outcomes for youth with disabilities (Crane & Mooney, 2005; Tindle, Leconte, Buchanan, & Taymans, 2005). It provides a systematic way of: (a) determining what already exists in the community that might align with students' interests, goals, and needs; and (b) making this information accessible and available to students, families, and the professionals who support them.

The process begins by assembling a "community mapping" team of individuals from within and beyond the school who collectively see their community from different vantage points. The team works together to assemble a list of all of the disability-specific and generically available programs and supports available to any young person in the local community. These entries are then organized by domain (e.g., employment, transportation, recreation and leisure, volunteering, civic involvement, residential) and each is accompanied by a resource description and contact information. The information is then compiled in accessible formats (e.g., print, website, downloadable guide, searchable database) and shared with members of all students' transition teams. At transition planning meetings, the community map might be drawn upon when deciding which community activities might interest the student, where skill instruction might best be delivered, or how a student's community involvement might be supported. High schools and school districts have successfully used community mapping to connect students with disabilities to a range of recreational and employment opportunities during the summer months when school is not in session (Carter, Trainor, Ditchman, Swedeen, & Owens, 2009). Community maps should be living documents that are updated over time as new opportunities and resources are identified.

Table 8.3. Developing Picture, Audio, and Video Self-Operated Prompting Systems

Steps	Self-operated picture prompting system	Self-operated audio prompting system	Self-operated video prompting system
1	Identify the target task.	Identify the target task.	Identify the target task.
2	Develop a task analysis.	Develop a task analysis.	Develop a task analysis.
3	Determine types of pictures to use (drawings, photos).	Determine "script" of auditory prompts.	Determine if student will use video prompting or video modeling.[a]
4	Identify words (if any) that will accompany pictures.	Determine who will be the "voice" on the audio system (student, teacher, favorite paraprofessional, parent) or whether a tone will be used to prompt the student to the next step.	Decide video point of view: Will it be from the student's perspective? Will it depict the student or a known or an unknown individual engaged in the task?
5	Identify how pictures will be presented (e.g., communication notebook, electronic system such as an iPad or on a computer).	Determine the system for delivering auditory prompts: Does it need to be portable? MP3 player? Smartphone? Laptop? Will headphones be needed?	Identify the system for delivering videos (DVD player, computer, iPad, iPhone).
6	Develop prompting system and ask two novel individuals to complete the task using the self-operated system. Make edits based on individuals' performance.	Develop prompting system and ask two novel individuals to complete the task using the self-operated system. Make edits based on individuals' performance.	Develop prompting system and ask two novel individuals to complete the task using the self-operated system. Make edits based on individuals' performance.

Table 8.3. Developing Picture, Audio, and Video Self-Operated Prompting Systems (cont'd)

Steps	Self-operated picture prompting system	Self-operated audio prompting system	Self-operated video prompting system
7	Determine if students will use self-management skills when using the self-operated system. Will students self-monitor their progress using a checklist? Will they engage in self-evaluation?	Determine if students will use self-management skills when using the self-operated system. Will students self-monitor their progress using a checklist? Will they engage in self-evaluation?	Determine if students will use self-management skills when using the self-operated system. Will students self-monitor their progress using a checklist? Will they engage in self-evaluation?
8	Evaluate student performance as they use the self-operated system.	Evaluate student performance as they use the self-operated system.	Evaluate student performance as they use the self-operated system.

Note. Adapted from *Footsteps Toward the Future: Implementing a Real-World Curriculum for Students With Disabilities,* by E. C. Bouck, T. Taber-Doughty, and M. N. Savage, 2015, p. 35. Copyright 2015 by Council for Exceptional Children.

[a] Video modeling refers to when a student completes a task after watching the whole video of the task; video prompting refers to when a student completes each step of a task after watching each component step of a task on video before moving on to the next step (see Cannella-Malone et al., 2011).

Community Conversations

Another promising approach for identifying new supports and community opportunities is through hosting a "community conversation" event. A *community conversation* is an asset-based approach for identifying and engaging a diverse group of local stakeholders in addressing the needs of transition-age youth and young adults (Carter & Bumble, 2018; Carter, Owens, et al., 2009). This structured approach to community dialogue draws upon the World Café model (Brown & Isaacs, 2005) to identify a wide range of informal and formal solutions and partners that could be drawn upon to improve the in- and postschool outcomes of students with disabilities. A local planning team identifies and invites a cross-section of diverse community members (e.g., civic leaders, educators, employers, students with disabilities, parents, disability professionals) to a 2-hour community conversation event. As many as 40 to 80 attendees participate in three rounds of small-group conversations during which they identify ideas, resources, opportunities, and personal connections that could be drawn upon to support effective transitions and community engagement for students with disabilities. Between each round of discussion, attendees switch tables and continue the conversation with a new combination of neighbors. The event culminates with a whole-group discussion in which attendees share the most promising possibilities and actionable strategies they heard throughout the event. The detailed notes taken at tables throughout the event are later compiled to provide a roadmap of the possible pathways and partners in the community that can be drawn upon to support transition-age youth with disabilities. The information gathered during the event can also be folded into the community mapping process. Schools, disability organizations, and families have used this approach to identify possibilities and partners in areas as diverse as integrated employment (Carter, Blustein, et al., 2016), independent living (Bumble, Carter, Gajjar, & Valentini, 2017), faith community involvement (Carter, Bumble, Griffin, & Curcio, 2017), postsecondary education (Bumble, Carter, Bethune, Day, & McMillan, 2018), and community recreation (Carter, Swedeen, Cooney, Walter, & Moss, 2012).

Developing Creative Community Partnerships

As new opportunities for community inclusion and instruction are identified, it is wise to pursue new partnerships with others in the community to support the active involvement of students with disabilities. Schools often struggle to establish relationships beyond formal agencies and organizations (e.g., vocational rehabilitation, independent living centers, employment providers, disabilities agencies, benefits counseling, mental health services). This section highlights avenues through which schools can cultivate partnerships that supplement their collaborations with service systems.

Employers and Business Networks

As students transition to adulthood, the world of work becomes a primary pathway for community participation. A good job provides a chance to contribute to the community, make social connections, and to acquire resources for other types of community involvement. As addressed in the chapter on employment, partnerships with individual businesses are essential to provide places for students to participate in internships, apprenticeships, and work-based learning. Yet many special educators feel poorly prepared to identify and invite employers into these important school-based partnerships (Kim & Dymond, 2010; Trainor, Carter, Owens, & Swedeen, 2008). Identifying someone to serve in the role of "community connector" may facilitate employer relations. This role involves identifying local job opportunities that align with students' vocational interests, contacting local employers about job openings and partnerships, assisting students in applying and interviewing for these jobs, and arranging needed on-the-job supports (Carter, Owens, et al., 2009). Likewise, some high schools identify someone on the business side to serve as an "employer liaison" whose role is to draw upon existing networks and relationships to help community connectors make linkages between students' interests and local employment, internship, or volunteer opportunities.

There are also advantages to establishing partnerships with networks of employers, like the local chamber of commerce or other associations of businesses invested in promoting the economic interests of the local community. Such groups typically represent a broad range of industry sectors and community organizations, provide extensive networking opportunities, share economic forecast information with the community, and support local groups. Partnering with these employer networks can give secondary schools access to a much broader range of potential employers while exponentially expanding the job opportunities, resources, and relationships available to students with developmental disabilities. Such employer networks may also be willing to support the career development of students by sharing job opportunities with schools, advocating for member businesses to hire students with disabilities, inviting schools to advocate for their students and supports at network meetings, and connecting educators to numerous local employers (Carter, Trainor, Cakiroglu, et al., 2009).

Civic and Community Groups

The importance of social capital for students with disabilities and their families has been much discussed in the transition literature (Carter, Sweeden, et al., 2012; Trainor, 2008). But the relationships transition teams cultivate with others in the community can also be instrumental to the success of students. When it comes to supporting community participation well, it matters who educators know. Efforts to develop new relationships with individual employers, volunteer coordinators, recreation program leaders, and others can be quite valuable, but difficult to undertake in the midst of limited time (Trainor et al., 2008). On the other hand, building connections with existing community groups can expand a school's network of potential partners, allies, and advocates. Even fairly small communities are home to a number of service, fraternal, civic, leadership, and charitable groups. Examples include Kiwanis, Moose, Rotary, Lions, Optimists, Exchange, Knights of Columbus, and many others. These groups often strive to support community initiatives, involve community leaders, and have members who have connections to almost every corner of the community. Inviting them to visit a school's program or offering to speak at their gatherings about transition can be a catalyst for developing new and lasting relationships.

Faith Communities

As is true for many Americans, spirituality and religious involvement is an important aspect of life for students with disabilities and their families (Boehm, Carter, & Taylor, 2015; Liu, Carter, Boehm, Annandale, & Taylor, 2014). Congregations often provide their members an array of opportunities to develop and deepen relationships, serve others, take classes, and develop one's talents and gifts. Yet many youth and young adults with disabilities are not invited or supported to participate to the extent they would like. Transition educators can: (a) provide interested parents with information about how to connect with and advocate for congregational supports that enable their child to participate in worship, learning, and fellowship activities offered by area faith groups; and (b) serve as resources to congregations interested in knowing how to best support their students (Carter, Boehm, Annandale, & Taylor, 2016).

In addition to supporting participation in congregational life, faith communities can also play a role in supporting other transition outcomes. For example, faith communities can help connect their members with disabilities to jobs by drawing upon the personal networks of congregation members, encouraging members to advocate within their own workplace, advocating for better community employment programs and supports, finding mentors willing to come alongside others through the job search, arranging transportation to work, and even hiring people within the congregation (Carter, Bumble, et al., 2017). This approach draws upon the social capital, creativity, and commitment within a congregation to connect the gifts and talents of people with disabilities to meaningful work (Carter, Endress, et al., 2016). Likewise, faith-based communities can make innovative contributions to supporting inclusive residential options, recreation involvement, community volunteering, and postsecondary education (Carter, 2011; Floding, 2012).

Families

Families often comprise the most prominent and enduring sources of natural support, advocacy, and guidance for students with disabilities. Although the extent to which parents, siblings, and other relatives will participate directly in the transition process will vary, family engagement remains a hallmark of best practices in transition education (Landmark, Ju, & Zhang, 2010). Several steps can be taken to enhance this engagement. First, transition teams can work to elevate their vision for future possibilities after high school. The expectations parents hold for work, college, and other postschool outcomes are among the most powerful predictors of their children actually attaining those outcomes (Carter, Austin, & Trainor, 2012; Simonsen & Neubert, 2013). Second, families can benefit from having help connecting to the array of formal and generically available programs that might assist them and their family members with disabilities during the transition years. Third, many parents have reported considerable difficulty finding accessible information related to their child's needs and postschool interests (Gilson, Bethune, Carter, & McMillan, 2017). Providing or connecting parents to reliable and relevant information can equip them with the tools they need to support their child well.

CASE STUDY 8.1 (Ms. Nowak)

Ms. Nowak is a high school special education teacher. She teaches a cross-categorical program focused on preparing her high school students for transition, employment, independent living, and life skills; in other words, real-world skills. Ms. Nowak is committed to teaching her students these skills in the most inclusive and natural settings. To establish these natural settings, Ms. Nowak has built meaningful community partnerships, including with local businesses and employers in her town as well as other community groups. To provide instruction in these skills in their natural settings, Ms. Nowak works to implement evidence-based practices, including systematic instruction and technology-aided instruction. For example, one of Ms. Nowak's students, Beth, interns at the public library in town helping to restock library shelves (i.e., return books to their correct location). To support Beth's employment skill success, Ms. Nowak created a video model as a means of providing a self-operated prompting tool to increase the Beth's independence and accuracy in obtaining and demonstrating the job skills. Ms. Nowak also sought to support Beth's independent employment potential by building generalization into teaching Beth how to return the book to the correct location. To do so, Ms. Nowak had Beth practice the same skills in the school's library as well as the local bookstore. The opportunities for Beth to intern at the public library and as well as practice her generalization of the skill at the local bookstore were a result of Ms. Nowak's continued effort to develop networks and partnerships within her local community. Ms. Nowak is committed to not only her students' success but also to being part of an inclusive community.

Summary

It is important to involve students with developmental disabilities, including those with autism spectrum disorder and intellectual disability in their broader community to the greatest extent possible. Youth and young adults with disabilities should receive real-life skills instruction within naturally occurring community-based settings. Likewise, youth and young adults with disabilities should be included in community activities and networks with a range of community members forged to develop and support these students' involvement. To help support transition and a more inclusive adult society and life for youth and young adults with disabilities, educators must take active roles in teaching real-life skills, do so in community-based settings to the maximum extent possible, and develop community partnerships and involve community members in the education programming of youth and young adults with disabilities.

References

Amado, A., Stancliffe, R. J., McCarron, M., & McCallion, P. (2013). Social inclusion and community participation of individuals with intellectual/developmental disabilities. *Inclusion, 51*, 360–375. doi:10.1352/1934-9556-51.5.360

Ayres, K. M., Lowrey, K. A., Douglas, K. H., & Sievers, C. (2011). I can identify Saturn but I can't brush my teeth: What happens when the curricular focus for students with severe disabilities shifts. *Education and Training in Autism and Developmental Disabilities, 46*, 11–21.

Ayres, K., M., Mechling, L., & Sansosti, F. J. (2013). The use of mobile technologies to assist with life skills/independence of students with moderate/severe intellectual disability and/or autism spectrum disorders: Considerations for the future of school psychology. *Psychology in the Schools, 50*, 259–270. doi:10.1002/pits.21673

Boehm, T. L., Carter, E. W., & Taylor, J. L. (2015). Factors associated with family quality of life during the transition to adulthood for youth and young adults with developmental disabilities. *American Journal on Intellectual and Developmental Disabilities, 120*, 395–411. doi:10.1352/1944-7558-120.5.395.

Bouck, E. C. (2012). Secondary curriculum and transition. In P. Wehman (Eds.), *Life beyond the classroom: Transition strategies for young people with disabilities* (5th ed., pp. 215–233). Baltimore, MD: Paul H. Brookes.

Bouck, E. C. (2017a). *Assistive technology*. Thousand Oaks, CA: SAGE.

Bouck, E. C. (2017b). Educational outcomes for secondary students with mild intellectual disability. *Education and Training in Autism and Developmental Disabilities, 54*, 369–382.

Bouck, E. C., Satsangi, R., & Bartlett, W. (2016). Comparing a number line and audio prompts in supporting price comparison by students with intellectual disability. *Research in Developmental Disabilities, 51*, 27–40. doi:10.1016/j.ridd.2016.02.011

Bouck, E. C., Savage, M., Meyer, N. K., Taber-Doughty, T., & Hunley, M. (2014). High-tech or low-tech? Comparing self-monitoring systems to increase task independence for students with autism. *Focus on Autism and Other Developmental Disabilities, 29*, 156–167. doi:10.1177/1088357614528797

Bouck, E. C., Taber-Doughty, T., & Savage, M. (2015). *Footsteps toward the future: A real-world focus for students with intellectual disability, autism spectrum disorder, and other developmental disabilities*. Arlington, VA: Council for Exceptional Children.

Browder, D. M., & Snell, M. E. (1993). Functional academics. In M. E. Snell (Ed.), *Instruction of students with severe disabilities* (4th ed., pp. 442–475). New York, NY: Merrill.

Browder, D. M., Wood, L., Thompson, J., & Ribuffo, C. (2014, August). *Evidence-based practices for students with severe disabilities* (CEEDAR Document No. IC-3). Gainesville: University of Florida, Collaboration for Effective Educator, Development, Accountability, and Reform Center. Retrieved from http://ceedar.education.ufl.edu/wp-content/uploads/2014/09/IC-3_FINAL_03-03-15.pdf

Brown, J., & Isaacs, D. (2005). *The world café: Shaping our futures through conversations that matter*. San Francisco, CA: Barrett-Koehler.

Brown, L., McLean, M. B., Hamre-Nietupski, S., Pumpian, I., Creto, N., & Gruenewald, L. (1979). A strategy for developing chronological age-appropriate and functional curricular content for severely handicapped adolescents and young adults. *The Journal of Special Education, 13*, 81–90. doi:10.1177/002246697901300113

Bumble, J. L., Carter, E. W., Bethune, L., Day, T., & McMillan, E. (2018). *Community conversations on inclusive higher education for students with intellectual disability*. Manuscript submitted for publication.

Bumble, J. L., Carter, E. W., Gajjar, S., & Valentini, B. (2017). *Understanding and supporting independent living: Findings from community conversations*. Manuscript in preparation.

Cannella-Malone, H. I., Fleming, C., Chung, Y-C., Wheeler, G. M., Basbagill, A. R., & Singh, A. H. (2011). Teaching daily living skills to seven individuals with severe intellectual disabilities: A comparison of video prompting to video modeling. *Journal of Positive Behavior Interventions, 13*, 144–153. doi:10.1177/1098300710266593

Carter, E. W. (2011). After the benediction: Walking alongside people with significant disabilities and their families in faith and life. *Journal of Religion, Disability, and Health, 15*, 395–413. doi:10.1080/15228967.2011.619340

Carter, E. W., Austin, D., & Trainor, A. A. (2012). Predictors of postschool employment outcomes for young adults with severe disabilities. *Journal of Disability Policy Studies, 23*, 50–63. doi:10.1177/1044207311414680

Carter, E. W., Blustein, C. L., Bumble, J. L., Harvey, S., Henderson, L., & McMillan, E. (2016). Engaging communities in identifying local strategies for expanding integrated employment during and after high school. *American Journal on Intellectual and Developmental Disabilities, 121*, 398–418. doi:10.1352/1944-7558-121.5

Carter, E. W., Boehm, T. L., Annandale, N. H., & Taylor, C. (2016). Supporting congregational inclusion for children and youth with disabilities and their families. *Exceptional Children, 82*, 372–389. doi:10.1177/0014402915598773

Carter, E. W., & Bumble, J. L. (2018). The promise and possibilities of community conversations: Expanding employment opportunities for people with disabilities. *Journal of Disability Policy Studies, 28,* 195–202. doi:10.1177/1044207317739408

Carter, E. W., Bumble, J. L., Griffin, B., & Curcio, M. P. (2017). Community conversations on faith and disability: Identifying new practices, postures, and partners for congregations. *Pastoral Psychology, 66*, 575–594. doi:10.1007/s11089-017-0770-4

Carter, E. W., Ditchman, N., Sun, Y., Trainor, A. A., Swedeen, B., & Owens, L. (2010). Summer employment and community experiences of transition-age youth with severe disabilities. *Exceptional Children, 76*, 194–212. doi:10.1177/001440291007600204

Carter, E. W., Endress, T., Gustafson, J., Shouse, J., Taylor, C., Utley, A., ... Allen, W. (2016). *Putting faith to work: A guide for congregations and communities on connecting job seekers with disabilities to meaningful work*. Nashville, TN: Collaborative on Faith and Disability.

Carter, E. W., Owens, L., Swedeen, B., Trainor, A. A., Thompson, C., Ditchman, N., & Cole, O. (2009). Conversations that matter: Expanding employment opportunities for youth with significant disabilities through community conversations. *TEACHING Exceptional Children, 41*(6), 38–46. doi:10.1177/004005990904100603

Carter, E. W., Swedeen, B., Cooney, M., Walter, M. J., & Moss, C. K. (2012). "I don't have to do this by myself?" Parent-led community conversations to promote inclusion. *Research and Practice for Persons with Severe Disabilities, 37*, 9–23. doi:10.2511/027494812800903184

Carter, E. W., Trainor, A. A., Cakiroglu, O., Cole, O., Swedeen, B., Ditchman, N., & Owens, L. (2009). Exploring school-business partnerships to expand career development and early work experiences for youth with disabilities. *Career Development for Exceptional Individuals, 32*, 145–159. doi:10.1177/0885728809344590

Carter, E. W., Trainor, A. A., Ditchman, N., Swedeen, B., & Owens, L. (2009). Evaluation of a multi-component intervention package to increase summer work experiences for transition-age youth with severe disabilities. *Research and Practice for Persons with Severe Disabilities, 34*, 1–12. doi:10.2511/rpsd.34.2.1

Clark, G. M., Field, S., Patton, J., Brolin, D., & Sitlington, P. (1994). Life skills instruction: A necessary component for all students with disabilities. *Career Developmental for Exceptional Individuals, 17*, 125–134. doi:10.1177/088572889401700202

Collins, B. C., Karl, J., Riggs, L., Galloway, C. C., & Hager, K. D. (2010). Teaching core content with real-life applications to secondary students with moderate and severe disabilities. *TEACHING Exceptional Children, 43*(1), 52–59. doi:10.1177/004005991004300106

Crane, K., & Mooney, M. (2005, May). *Community resource mapping* (Essential Tools: Improving Secondary Education and Transition for Youth With Disabilities). Minneapolis, MN: National Center on Secondary Education and Transition.

Cronin, M. E., & Patton, J. R. (1993). *Life skills instruction for all students with special needs: A practical guide for integrating real-life content into the curriculum.* Austin, TX: PRO-ED.

Dattilo, J., & Hoge, G. (1999). Effects of a leisure education program on youth with mental retardation. *Education and Training in Mental Retardation and Developmental Disabilities, 34*, 20–34.

Floding, M. (2012). *Lessons from Friendship House. Faith and Leadership.* Retrieved from www.friendshiphousepartners.org

Gajar, A., Goodman, L., & McAfee, J. (1993). *Secondary schools and beyond: Transition of individuals with mild disabilities.* New York, NY: Merrill.

Gilson, C. B., Bethune, L., Carter, E. W., & McMillan, E. (2017). Informing and equipping parents of people with intellectual and developmental disabilities. *Intellectual and Developmental Disabilities, 43*, 20–37. doi:10.1177/1540796917751134

Hong, E. R., Ganz, J. B., Mason, R., Morin, K., Davis, J. L., Ninci, J., … Gilliland, W. D. (2016). The effects of video modeling in teaching functional living skills to persons with ASD: A meta-analysis of single case studies. *Research in Developmental Disabilities, 57*, 158–169. doi:10.1016/j.ridd.2016.07.001

Hughes, C., & Carter, E. W. (2011). Transition supports: Equipping youth for adult life. *Journal of Vocational Rehabilitation, 35*, 177–180. doi:10.3233/JVR-2011-0567

Kim, R., & Dymond, S. K. (2010). Special education teachers' perceptions of benefits, barriers, and components of community-based vocational instruction. *Intellectual and Developmental Disabilities, 48*, 313–329. doi:10.1352/1934-9556-48.5.313

Kolstoe, O. P. (1970). *Teaching educable mentally retarded children*. New York, NY: Holt, Rinehart, & Winston.

Landmark, L. J., Ju, S., & Zhang, D. (2010). Substantiated best practices in transition: Fifteen plus years later. *Career Development for Exceptional Individuals, 33*, 165–176. doi:10.1177/0885728810376410

Liu, E. X., Carter, E. W., Boehm, T. L., Annandale, N., & Taylor, C. (2014). In their own words: The place of faith in the lives of young people with intellectual disability and autism. *Intellectual and Developmental Disabilities, 52*, 388–404. doi:10.1352/1934-9556-52.5.388

Mazzotti, V. L., Rowe, D. A., Cameto, R., Test, D. W., & Morningstar, M. E. (2013). Identifying and promoting transition evidence-based practices and predictors of success: A position paper of the Division on Career Development and Transition. *Career Development and Transition for Exceptional Individuals, 36*, 140–151. doi:10.1177/2165143413503365

Mechling, L. C., Gast, D. L., & Seid, N. H. (2010). Evaluation of a personal digital assistant as a self-prompting device for increasing multi-step task completion by students with moderate intellectual disabilities. *Education and Training in Autism and Developmental Disabilities, 45*, 422–439.

Retish, P., Hitchings, W., Horvath, M., & Schmalle, B. (1991). *Students with mild disabilities in the secondary school*. New York, NY: Longman.

Sands, D. J., & Doll, B. (1996). Fostering self-determination is a developmental task. *The Journal of Special Education, 30*, 58–76. doi:10.1177/002246699603000104

Seward, J., Schuster, J. W, Ault, M. J., Collins, B. C., & Hall, M. (2014). Comparing simultaneous prompting and constant time delay to teach leisure skills to students with moderate intellectual disability. *Education and Training in Autism and Developmental Disabilities, 49*, 381–395.

Shurr, J., Jimenez, B., & Bouck, E. C. (Eds.). (in press). *Evidence-based practices for educating students with intellectual disability and autism spectrum disorder*. Arlington, VA: Council for Exceptional Children.

Simonsen, M. L., & Neubert, D. A. (2013). Transitioning youth with intellectual and other developmental disabilities: Predicting community employment outcomes. *Career Development and Transition for Exceptional Individuals, 36*, 188–198. doi:10.1177/2165143412469399

Snell, M., & Browder, D. (1987). Domestic and community skills. In M. Snell (Ed.), *Systematic instruction of persons with severe handicaps* (pp. 390–434). Columbus, OH: Merrill.

Spooner, F., Browder, D. M., & Mims, P. (2011). Evidence-based practices. In D. M. Browder & F. Spooner (Eds.), *Teaching students with moderate and severe disabilities* (pp. 92–125). New York, NY: Guilford.

Storey, K., & Miner, C. (2011). *Systematic instruction of functional skills for students and adults with disabilities*. Springfield, IL: Charles C. Thomas.

Test, D. W., Fowler, C. H., Richter, S., White, J. A., Mazzotti, V. L., Walker, A. R., … Kortering, L. (2009). Evidence-based practices in secondary transition. *Career Development for Exceptional Individuals, 32*, 115–128. doi:10.1177/0885728809336859

Test, D. W., Smith, L., & Carter, E. W. (2014). Equipping youth with autism spectrum disorders for adulthood: Promoting rigor, relevance, and relationships. *Remedial and Special Education, 35*, 80–90. doi:10.1177/0741932513514857

Test, D. W., Spooner, F., Holzberg, D., Roberston, C., & Davis, L. L. (2016). Planning for other educational needs and community-based instruction. In M. L. Wehmeyer, & K. A. Shogren (Eds.), *Handbook of research-based practices for educating students with intellectual disability* (pp. 130–150). New York, NY: Routledge.

Tindle, K., Leconte, P., Buchanan, L., & Taymans, J. M. (2005). Transition planning: Community mapping as a tool for teachers and students. *Research to Practice Brief, 4*, 1–6.

Trainor, A. A. (2008). Using cultural and social capital to improve postsecondary outcomes and expand transition models for youth with disabilities. *The Journal of Special Education, 42*, 148–162. doi:10.1177/0022466907313346

Trainor, A. A., Carter, E. W., Owens, L., & Swedeen, B. (2008). Special educators' perceptions of summer employment and community participation opportunities for youth with disabilities. *Career Development for Exceptional Individuals, 31*, 144–153. doi:10.1177/0885728808323717

Wehmeyer, M. L., Sands, D. J., Knowlton, H. E., & Kozleski, E. B. (2002). *Providing access to the general curriculum: Teaching students with mental retardation*. Baltimore, MD: Paul H. Brookes.

Westling, D. L., & Fox, L. (2000). *Teaching students with severe disabilities* (2nd ed.). Upper Saddle, NJ: Merrill.

Wong, C., Odom, S., Hume, K. A., Cox, A. W., Fettig, A., Kucharczyk, S., ... Schultz, T. R. (2015). Evidence-based practices for children, youth, and young adults with autism spectrum disorder: A comprehensive review. *Journal of Autism and Developmental Disorders, 45*, 1951–1966. doi:10.1007/s10803-014-2351-z

Index

Symbols
21st-century skills 67, 69, 71
2004 authorization 23

A
adaptive behavior(s) 4, 25, 26, 30, 105
adaptive coaching/coaches 12, 13, 72–75, 110, 114
adult roles 5, 6, 10, 13, 14, 36
adult service provider(s) 37, 85, 90, 91
age-appropriate roles 12, 53
Americans With Disabilities Act (and ADAAA) 7, 9, 80, 99

B
barriers to employment 82, 83, 86
Best Buddies 131
bridges from school to working life 21, 22

C
choice making 25, 43
circles of support 59, 61
citizenship 60
civic and community groups 135
collaborative teaming 11, 12, 70
communication (skills) 3, 13, 39, 40, 57, 68, 71, 73, 74, 83, 105, 115, 132
community-based instruction 2, 89, 125, 126, 130
community conversations 126, 131, 133
community living 5, 6, 7, 8, 10–14, 36, 37, 39, 50, 51, 55, 60
community mapping 85, 126, 131, 134
community participation 2, 5, 14, 51, 52, 57, 125, 126, 130, 134, 135
community services 55
community supports 60, 131
competitive integrated employment 2, 9, 44, 79–81, 90, 91
criterion of normalization 21
criterion of ultimate functioning 21, 22
customized employment 80, 81, 90

D
daily living (skills) 5, 59, 61, 69, 126–128
decision making (skills) 12, 25, 43, 53, 60, 61, 87, 108
deinstitutionalization movement of the 1960s and 1970s 8
disability rights movement 20

E

Education for All Handicapped Children Act 23
emotional regulation 82, 105
employment opportunities 22, 26, 28, 40, 72, 80, 90, 131
employment settings 26, 53, 82
evidence-based strategies 2, 10, 14, 35, 69, 79
expectations 11, 13, 24, 61, 71, 73, 74, 83, 105, 106, 136
  high expectations 56, 67, 75, 85, 101
  low expectations 82
experiential assessment 87, 89, 90
extended transition services 43, 44
extracurricular activities 85, 99, 102

F

faith communities 136
family engagement 136
formal transition assessments 24, 25
free and appropriate education 23, 56
"front door first" approach 12, 51, 53, 72, 75
functional curriculum 70, 127
functional living skills 69

G

goal setting (skills) 43, 87, 108, 111
graduation rate 70
guardianship 2, 49, 50, 58–62

H

Halpern, Andrew 6, 7, 42
healthy living 60

I

inclusion 12, 38, 53, 68, 69, 71, 72, 75, 83, 85, 99, 101, 103, 104, 116, 130, 134
inclusive curricula/curriculum 8, 69, 70, 72
inclusive education 21, 51, 69, 94
inclusive opportunities 10, 12, 72
inclusive settings 2, 10, 67–69, 72
independent living 4, 5, 22–24, 29, 38, 39, 40, 44, 57, 63, 68, 72, 80, 101, 110, 115, 116, 126–128, 134, 137, 139
individualized education program, IEP 4, 7–9, 23–25, 36, 37, 41, 42, 44, 54, 56–58, 62, 69, 85, 105–109
individualized plan for employment, IPE 35, 36
individualized service plan, ISP 36, 43
Individuals With Disabilities Education Act 1, 3, 9, 23, 36, 56, 70, 80, 99
  1997 amendments 7, 23
  2004 reauthorization 7, 23

informal transition assessments 23, 25, 26
informed consent 58
integrated employment 2, 5, 9, 13, 14, 23, 36, 44, 68, 79–81, 88, 90, 91
interagency agreement 37
interagency collaboration/partnerships 8, 36–38, 41, 44, 72
interest inventory/inventories 25, 26
internship 39, 42, 43, 73, 88, 89, 103, 134, 135
interpersonal (interactions, skills) 83

L

literacy 14, 73, 82, 108, 127

M

mental health services 116, 134
misperceptions (about people with disabilities) 82
model demonstration(s) 10, 72

N

National Collaborative on Workforce and Disability for Youth 44
National Longitudinal Transition Study 81, 107
National Secondary Transition Technical Assistance Center 40, 56
National Transition Documentation Summit 56
natural environment 22, 125
natural supports 12, 13, 50, 51, 53, 72–75, 90, 110

O

Office of Special Education Programs, OSEP 6
on-the-job supports 135
on-the-job training 90
organization (skills) 73, 105, 108

P

paid employment 39, 43, 68
parent involvement 83
perceptions, negative 82
person-centered planning 2, 10, 11, 36, 49, 50, 52–55, 85, 89, 103, 107, 110
person-first language 8
positive employment outcomes, predictors of 83, 84
postschool outcomes, predictors of 37–40, 42, 68, 81, 133, 136
postsecondary education 5, 7, 8, 10, 13
postsecondary goals 4, 20, 23, 24, 29, 36, 50, 56, 57, 62
postsecondary transition plan 23
power of attorney 60
preferences, interests, needs, and strengths – student's 11, 20, 23, 24, 29, 36, 85, 87, 110, 114
principle of normalization 21, 22
problem solving (skills) 43, 108

R

real-life settings 71
real-life skills 2, 125–128, 130, 138
real-world skills 14, 125, 137
Rehabilitation Act of 1973 7, 36, 80, 99
repeated measures situational assessment 19, 20, 25–29

S

safety 14, 60, 61, 108, 109, 125, 127
School to-Work Opportunity Act 80
segregation 20, 82
self-advocacy 12, 13, 39, 43, 53, 71, 72, 80, 89, 101, 107, 108, 116
self-awareness 43, 108
self-determination 10, 11, 12, 25, 26, 35, 39, 40, 43, 44, 57, 60, 68, 70, 72, 73, 79, 83, 86, 101, 106–108, 126–128
self-determined 11, 43, 67, 70, 71
self-directed assessments 26
self-management 43, 73, 108, 133
self-regulation 12, 39
self-sufficiency 4, 85, 91
service delivery, levels of 5
service systems 134
skills
   academic 13, 67–71, 73–75, 82, 108, 126–128
   nonacademic 13, 69–71, 75, 108
social interaction/socialization 3, 13, 68, 74, 111, 114, 125
social isolation 79
social skills 39, 57, 73, 85, 106, 115
soft skills 68, 72
special education, purpose of 23
special needs trust 61
Special Olympics 131
standards-based instruction 128
stigma 8, 20, 79, 82
student involvement/participation 23, 35, 42, 44
Summary of Performance (SOP) 2, 49, 50, 53, 56–58, 62, 108
Supplemental Security Income 61
supported decision making 61, 63
supported employment 5, 35, 36, 55, 90
systematic instruction 128, 129, 137

T

Ticket to Work and Work Incentives Improvement Act 80
time management 73, 74, 127
transition assessment, IDEA requirements for 3, 7, 9, 23, 29, 36
transition assessment, types of 24, 29
transition goals 12, 37, 57, 81, 107

transition IEP 107
transition (outcome) domains 23–25, 51–54
transition planning process 23, 29, 39, 87

V

video modeling 130, 132, 133
vocational education 5, 7, 40, 126, 127
vocational rehabilitation 1, 35–37, 42, 43, 57, 58, 71, 80, 86, 88 89, 134

W

wage disparity 81
Will, Madeline 5
work experience(s) 27–29, 37, 39, 40, 43, 44, 68, 81, 82, 83, 85, 88, 89, 91
Workforce Innovation and Opportunity Act 36, 80
work skills 80, 85
World Café model 133

Z

Zarrow Center for Learning Enrichment 24, 87